The Rudiments of Mandarin

中文初階

All MP3 audio files in the book can be downloaded at https://www.hkupress.hku.hk/+extras/1595audio/.

The Rudiments of Mandarin

中文初階

Yan Yan Chan Hong Yang Yuk Yeung Wei Zhang
陈欣欣　　 杨 虹　　 杨 煜　　 张 伟

Hong Kong University Press
The University of Hong Kong
Pokfulam Road
Hong Kong
www.hkupress.hku.hk

© 2018 Hong Kong University Press

ISBN 978-988-8390-95-3 (*Paperback*)

All rights reserved. No portion of this publication may be reproduced or transmitted in any form or by any means, electronic or mechanical, including photocopying, recording, or any information storage or retrieval system, without prior permission in writing from the publisher.

British Library Cataloguing-in-Publication Data
A catalogue record for this book is available from the British Library.

Calligraphy on the front cover by Cuncun Wu.

10 9 8 7 6 5 4 3 2 1

Printed and bound by Hang Tai Printing Co. Ltd., Hong Kong, China

Contents

Preface vi

Abbreviations vii

Introduction 1

Chapter 1　It's nice to meet you 8

Chapter 2　My family 22

Chapter 3　Shopping 38

Chapter 4　Where to eat 54

Chapter 5　My university life 68

Chapter 6　My roommate 82

Chapter 7　The weather 94

Chapter 8　Yin cha 110

Chapter 9　Reading week 126

Chapter 10　May I ask how to get to the library? 140

Appendix 1: Introduction to Chinese characters 155

Appendix 2: Read and write Chinese characters 159

Index 201

Preface

This textbook integrates principles and elements of Y. R. Chao's *Mandarin Primer* (1948) and *Chinese Primer* (Ta-Tuan Ch'en et al., 1989), both of which we admire, as well as feedback from our international students studying Chinese at the University of Hong Kong. We believe that students can acquire Chinese as a foreign language more effectively if they can apply the target language to daily life through a carefully organized framework of tonal pronunciation, grammar points, and vocabulary. Additionally, the text encourages students to communicate with teachers, classmates, and friends in Chinese, inside and outside the classroom, stressing the unity of the four basic skills of listening, speaking, reading, and writing—as well as the integration of language usage and context.

In order to help students internalize Chinese, the textbook begins by introducing the learner to the pinyin system and then provides realistic dialogs that contain a number of basic grammar points and key vocabulary. Chapter topics concerning student life on campus and in Hong Kong are drawn from student feedback on our courses and students' expressed wish to use a text with content that will help them communicate with Chinese people more efficiently. More specifically, students have indicated an interest in self-introduction, campus life, transportation, shopping, eating, and travel. Each chapter of this textbook consists of five sections: text, vocabulary, grammar, exercises, and culture notes. The introduction to pinyin and Chinese characters (in Appendix 1) is for beginning students. There are 130 basic but important grammar points and 400 common but simple vocabulary words in these ten chapters. Many of the commonly used terms concern Hong Kong society and culture. These sentence patterns and expressions are not intellectually difficult, and introducing them early allows students to quickly adapt to Mandarin as a living and natural language. There is a list of 300 Chinese characters from Chapters 1 to 10 in Appendix 2. Each character includes pinyin, its English meaning, and examples of common word usage. Students are encouraged to study these characters and the list of Chinese characters after they master the phonetic system and finish Chapter 1.

We have made every effort in this textbook to fill each lesson with cross-cultural communication experience of Chinese language learners. In addition, the textbook includes audio recordings of the text, vocabulary, and listening exercises. These will help students practice pronunciation and assimilate the dialogs. We also hope they will encourage students' engagement with the language in and out of class.

We wish to express our sincere gratitude to Professor Cuncun Wu; the project would not have been possible without her firm and constant support. We would like to sincerely thank Xiaoqian Cheng, Zhiyong Lu, Chen Chen, Xiaoyi Li, Li Hayden Hean Ting, and Mair Gareth James for their important assistance in the completion of the textbook. Their efforts have greatly enhanced the presentation of this text. We also appreciate the reviewers', Dr. Susie Han's, and Ms. Clara Ho's valuable suggestions and comments.

Abbreviations

adj. = adjective
adv. = adverb
conj. = conjunction
inter. = interjection
lit. = literally
m.w. = measure word
n. = noun

neg. = negative
num. = number
obj. = object
part. = sentence particle
pl. = plural
prep. = preposition
pron. = pronoun

p.w. = place word
q.w. = question word
subj. = subject
t.w. = time word
v. = verb
v.p. = verb phrase

Introduction

Hànyǔ pīnyīn (simply pinyin), the Chinese Phonetic System

1. Chinese syllables

A typical Chinese syllable includes three parts: initial letter(s), final letter(s), and a tone. For example:

Hè (贺, surname): "h" is the initial letter, "e" is the final letter, and " ` " indicates the tone.
Lǎoshī (老师, teacher): "l" and "sh" are the initial letters, "ao" and "i" are the final letters, " ˇ " and " ˉ " are the tones,

2. Chinese phonetic letters (hànyǔ pīnyīn letters)

声母 (shēng mǔ, initial letters)

b	p	m	f	d	t	n	l
g	k	h		j	q	x	
z	c	s		zh	ch	sh	r
y	w						

The letters "y" and "w" are supplementary initial letters. They are used as initial letters but pronounced as single final letters, "i" and "u" respectively.

韵母 (yùn mǔ, final letters)

单韵母 (dān yùn mǔ, single final letters):

| a | o | e | ê | i | u | ü |

复韵母 (fù yùn mǔ, compound final letters):

| ai | ei (êi) | ao | ou | uo | ie (iê) | üe (üê) |
| iu (iou) | ui (uei) | ia | iao | ua | uai | er |

Note: When "iou" and "uei" are used after the initial letter(s), they are written "iu" and "ui" respectively. For example: "qiu" is "qiou," and "cui" is "cuei."

鼻韵母 (bí yùn mǔ, nasal final letters):

-n:	an	en	in	ün			
-ng:	ang	eng	ing	ong			
	ian	iang	iong	uan	uang	un (uen)	üan

Note: When "uen" is a syllable, it is written "wen" (refer to the spelling rules). When "uen" is used after initial letter(s), it is written "un." For example: "s" + "uen" is written as "sun."

The important letters should be memorized:

a	o	e		i	u	ü			
b	p	m	f	d	t	n	l		
g	k	h		j	q	x			
z	c	s		zh	ch	sh	r		
ai	ei	ie	üe	ao	iu	ui	uo	ou	er
an	en	in	un	ün	ang	eng	ing	ong	

3. 声调 shēng diào (the tones)

There are five tones in modern Chinese. See details in the following table:

name	1st tone	2nd tone	3rd tone	4th tone	light tone
example	mā	má	mǎ	mà	ma

	First tone (55)	Second tone (35)	Third tone (214)	Fourth tone (51)
5 high				
4 mid-high				
3 middle				
2 mid-low				
1 low				

- The level of the first tone is "55" and marked " ˉ ".
- The level of the second tone is "35" and marked " ´ ".
- The level of third tone is "214" and marked " ˇ ". It is normally pronounced in half tones, which are mostly the first half, "212," and sometimes the second half, "24."
- The level of the fourth tone is "51" and marked " ` ".
- The light tone (also called soft tone/neutral tone) is light and short and appears only after one of the four tones above. No tone mark is needed.

A syllable changes its meaning when it is pronounced in different tones. Different characters may be pronounced in the same syllable and the same tone. For example:

mā: 妈 (mom)、抹 (wipe)...

má: 麻 (a general term for hemp, flax, jute, numb, coarse)...

mǎ: 马 (horse)、码 (code) . . .

mà: 骂 (curse, condemn) . . .

ma: 吗、嘛 (particle words)

(The same character may be pronounced in different syllables and/or different tones with different meanings.)

4. The spelling rules

I. As mentioned above, a typical syllable = initial letter(s) + final letter(s) + a tone. However, a syllable may contain only a final letter or letters but never an initial letter or letters alone. For example: ài (爱, love), áng (昂, raise up head).

II. Some initial letters (j q x, z c s, zh ch sh r, y) are indeed pronounced as syllables but must be spelled with "i." For example: jī qī xī, zī cī sī, zhī chī shī rì, yī.

III. Where is the tone marked?

(a) The tone mark is always used above one of the six simple final letters, based on the rule "first come, first marked" in the order of "a o e i u ü." For example: hǎo, hái, zuò, zǒu, xièxie.

(b) iu/ui: The tone mark always goes with the last letter. For example: huì, liú.

(c) When the tone is marked above "i," the dot is omitted. For example: yì, qǐ.

IV. "i," "u," and "ü" can never be used alone or at the beginning of a syllable.

If "i" and "u" are syllables by themselves, they are spelled "yi" and "wu" respectively.

If "i" and "u" are the first letters of the syllables, they are replaced by "y" and "w" respectively. For example: "ie" is spelled "ye"; "uo" is spelled "wo."

If "ü" is a syllable by itself or at the beginning of a syllable, "y" is used before it and the two dots over it are omitted. For example, "ü" is spelled "yu"; "üe" is spelled "yue."

Here is a summary of the spelling rules of these three letters:

Final	Syllable	Final	Syllable	Final	Syllable
i	yi	ü	yu	u	wu
ia	ya	üe	yue	ua	wa
ie	ye	üan	yuan	uo	wo
ian	yan	ün	yun	uai	wai
iao	yao			uei	wei
iou	you			uan	wan
iang	yang			uen	wen
in	yin			uang	wang
ing	ying			ueng	weng
iong	yong				

V. When "ü" appears after "y, j, q, x," the two dots above "ü" are omitted. For example, "yü" "jü" "qü" and "xü" are spelled "yu" "ju" "qu" and "xu" respectively.

VI. When the second syllable of a word begins with "a, o, e," a partition mark should be used to separate the two syllables of the word.

For example: Xī'ān (to differentiate from "Xiān"); Tiān'é (as opposed to "tiā né")

VII. Tone changes (biàndiào / sandhi)

a. Third-tone change (sān shēng biàndiào / sandhi)
When two 3rd tones appear together, the first 3rd tone is changed to the 2nd tone in pronunciation, but the tone mark normally does not change. For example, "Hello!" is written "Nǐ hǎo!" but pronounced "ní hǎo!"

When three 3rd tones appear together, the second 3rd tone is changed to the 2nd tone when pronounced, or both the first and the second 3rd tones are changed to the 2nd tone. For example, "I am very well" is written "wǒ hěn hǎo" but pronounced either "wǒ hén hǎo" or "wó hén hǎo."

b. "yī" (one, "一") tone change ("yī" biàndiào / sandhi)
When "一" is followed by the 1st, 2nd, and 3rd tones, it is usually pronounced in the 4th. When "一" is followed by the 4th tone, it is pronounced in the 2nd tone. For example:

"一" (yī)
- A day   : written "yītiān" but read "yì tiān"
- A year   : written "yīnián" but read "yì nián"
- A second : written "yīmiǎo" but read "yìmiǎo"
- A quarter : written "yīkè" but read "yíkè"

c. "bù" (not, "不") tone change ("bù" biàndiào / sandhi)
"不" is a 4th-tone syllable. When it is followed by another 4th-tone syllable, even if it is marked as 4th tone, it is pronounced as 2nd tone. For example, "is not" is written "bù shì" but pronounced "bú shì".

In our textbook, we indicate the actual pronunciation of "yī" and "bù" in order to make them perfectly clear.

VIII. The "er" suffix
"Er" ("儿") is sometimes attached to another syllable to form a retroflex syllable. For example, "哪儿" is read as one syllable, "nǎr," instead of two syllables, "nǎ ér," and means "where."

5. The sounds of the modern Chinese language

	a	o	e	-i	er	ai	ei	ao	ou	an	en	ang	eng	ong
b	ba	bo				bai	bei	bao		ban	ben	bang	beng	
p	pa	po				pai	pei	pao	pou	pan	pen	pang	peng	
m	ma	mo	me			mai	mei	mao	mou	man	men	mang	meng	
f	fa	fo				fai	fei		fou	fan	fen	fang	feng	
d	da		de			dai	dei	dao	dou	dan		dang	deng	dong
t	ta		te			tai		tao	tou	tan		tang	teng	tong
n	na		ne			nai	nei	nao	nou	nan	nen	nang	neng	nong
l	la		le			lai	lei	lao	lou	lan		lang	leng	long
g	ga		ge			gai	gei	gao	gou	gan	gen	gang	geng	gong
k	ka		ke			kai	kei	kao	kou	kan	ken	kang	keng	kong
h	ha		he			hai	hei	hao	hou	han	hen	hang	heng	hong
j														
q														
x														
z	za		ze	zi		zai	zei	zao	zou	zan	zen	zang	zeng	zong
c	ca		ce	ci		cai		cao	cou	can	cen	cang	ceng	cong
s	sa		se	si		sai		sao	sou	san	sen	sang	seng	song
zh	zha		zhe	zhi		zhai	zhei	zhao	zhou	zhan	zhen	zhang	zheng	zhong
ch	cha		che	chi		chai		chao	chou	chan	chen	chang	cheng	chong
sh	sha		she	shi		shai	shei	shao	shou	shan	shen	shang	sheng	
r			re	ri				rao	rou	ran	ren	rang	reng	rong
	a	o	e	-i	er	ai	ei	ao	ou	an	en	ang	eng	ong

	i	ia	iao	ie	iou	ian	in	iang	ing	iong
b	bi		biao	bie		bian	bin		bing	
p	pi		piao	pie		pian	pin		ping	
m	mi		miao	mie	miu	mian	min		ming	
f										
d	di		diao	die	diu	dian			ding	
t	ti		tiao	tie		tian			ting	
n	ni		niao	nie	niu	nian	nin	niang	ning	
l	li	lia	liao	lie	liu	lian	lin	liang	ling	
g										
k										
h										
j	ji	jia	jiao	jie	jiu	jian	jin	jiang	jing	jiong
q	qi	qia	qiao	qie	qiu	qian	qin	qiang	qing	qiong
x	xi	xia	xiao	xie	xiu	xian	xin	xiang	xing	xiong
z										
c										
s										
zh										
ch										
sh										
r										
	yi	ya	yao	ye	you	yan	yin	yang	ying	yong

	u	ua	uo	uai	uei	uan	uen	uang	ueng
b	bu								
p	pu								
m	mu								
f	fu								
d	du		duo		dui	duan	dun		
t	tu		tuo		tui	tuan	tun		
n	nu		nuo			nuan	lun		
l	lu		luo			luan			
g	gu	gua	guo	guai	gui	guan	gun	guang	
k	ku	kua	kuo	kuai	kui	kuan	kun	kuang	
h	hu	hua	huo	huai	hui	huan	hun	huang	
j									
q									
x									
z	zu		zuo		zui	zuan	zun		
c	cu		cuo		cui	cuan	cun		
s	su		suo		sui	suan	sun		
zh	zhu	zhua	zhuo	zhuai	zhui	zhuan	zhun	zhuang	
ch	chu	chua	chuo	chuai	chui	chuan	chun	chuang	
sh	shu	shua	shuo	shuai	shui	shuan	shun	shuang	
r	ru	rua	ruo		rui	ruan	run	ruang	
	wu	wa	wo	wai	wei	wan	wen	wang	weng

	ü	üe	üan	ün
b				
p				
m				
f				
d				
t				
n	nü	nüe		
l	lü	lüe		
g				
k				
h				
j	ju	jue	juan	jun
q	qu	que	quan	qun
x	xu	xue	xuan	xun
z				
c				
s				
zh				
ch				
sh				
r				
	yu	yue	yuan	yun

1
It's nice to meet you

Teacher : Hello everyone!
Students 1 and 2 : Hello teacher!
Teacher : My surname is Ding. I'm your Chinese teacher. What is your name?
Student 1 : My surname is also Ding. I am called Ding Yimei. I'm your student. I study law. Are you from China?
Teacher : Yes. Where are you from?

lǎoshī	老师	n.	teacher
nǐmen	你们	pron.	you (plural)
hǎo	好	adj.	good; fine; well
xuésheng	学生	n.	student
nín	您	pron.	you (in a respectful way)
wǒ	我	pron.	I; me
xìng	姓	n./v.	surname; surname is . . .
Dīng	丁	n.	a Chinese surname
yī	一	num.	one
měi	美	adj.	pretty; beautiful
shì	是	v.	to be; am; is; are
nǐmen de	你们的	pron.	your (phrase); yours

Dì-yī kè

Rènshi nǐmen hěn gāoxìng

Lǎoshī : Nǐmen[1] hǎo![2]
Xuésheng 1 and 2 : Nín hǎo!
Lǎoshī : Wǒ xìng[3] Dīng. Wǒ shì[4] nǐmen de[5] Hànyǔ lǎoshī.[6] Nǐ xìng shénme?[7]
Xuésheng 1 : Wǒ yě[8] xìng Dīng, jiào Dīng Yīměi. Wǒ shì nín de xuésheng. Wǒ xuéxí fǎlǜ zhuānyè. Nín shì Zhōngguó rén ma?[9]
Lǎoshī : Shì de.[10] Nǐ shì nǎ[11] guó rén?

Hànyǔ	汉语	n.	Chinese language
shénme	什么	pron.	what
yě	也	adv.	also; too
jiào	叫	v.	to be called
xuéxí	学习	v.	to study
fǎlǜ	法律	n.	law
zhuānyè	专业	n.	major
Zhōngguó	中国	n.	China; Chinese
rén	人	n.	person; people
ma	吗	part.	a sentence particle to indicate a question
shì de	是的		yes; you are right
nǎ	哪	pron.	which
guó	国	n.	country

Student 1 : I'm from Britain. (*Student 1 asks Student 2*.) What's your name?
Student 2 : My name is Wang Erming. I'm also a student of Teacher Ding.
Student 1 : Are you British?
Student 2 : No, I'm American.
Teacher : Do you also study law?
Student 2 : No, I study economics.
Teacher : Is your major difficult?
Student 2 : My major in economics is a bit challenging. (*Student 2 asks Student 1*.) How about your major?

Xuésheng 1： Wǒ shì Yīngguó rén. (*wèn xuésheng 2*) Nǐ jiào shénme míngzi?¹²
Xuésheng 2： Wǒ jiào Wáng Èrmíng, yě shì Dīng lǎoshī de xuésheng.
Xuésheng 1： Nǐ shì Yīngguó rén ma?
Xuésheng 2： Bù,¹³ wǒ shì Měiguó rén.
Lǎoshī ： Nǐ yě xuéxí fǎlǜ ma?
Xuésheng 2： Bú shì, wǒ xuéxí jīngjì.
Lǎoshī ： Nǐ de zhuānyè nán ma?
Xuésheng 2： Wǒ de zhuānyè tǐng nán de.¹⁴ (*wèn xuésheng 1*) Nǐ de zhuānyè ne?¹⁵

Yīngguó	英国	n.	Britain
míngzi	名字	n.	whole name
Wáng	王	n.	a Chinese surname
èr	二	num.	two
míng	明	adj.	clean; bright
bù	不		no; not
Měiguó	美国	n.	USA
jīngjì	经济	n.	economics
nán	难	adj.	difficult
tǐng……de	挺……的		quite; fairly
ne	呢	part.	how about

Student 1	: I'm majoring in law, which is very challenging. Teacher Ding, do you like teaching?
Teacher	: Yes, my job is very interesting. Nice to meet you.
Students 1 and 2	: Nice to meet you too. Good-bye!
Teacher	: Good-bye!

Xuésheng 1	:	Wǒ de zhuānyè hěn[16] nán. Dīng lǎoshī, nín de gōngzuò yǒu yìsi ma?	
Lǎoshī	:	Wǒ de gōngzuò fēicháng[17] yǒu yìsi. Rènshi nǐmen hěn gāoxìng.	
Xuésheng 1 and 2	:	Rènshi nín wǒmen yě hěn gāoxìng. Zàijiàn.[18]	
Lǎoshī	:	Zàijiàn.	

hěn	很	adv.	very
gōngzuò	工作	n./v.	job; to work
yǒu yìsi	有意思	adj.	interesting
fēicháng	非常	adv.	extraordinarily
rènshi	认识	n.	to know someone
gāoxìng	高兴	adj.	glad; happy
zàijiàn	再见		good-bye; see you

Grammar

1. Personal pronouns

Singular forms:

> nǐ : "you" (sing.); "nín" is a polite form of address for "you" in Chinese, especially in the northern part of China.
>
> wǒ : "I, me"
>
> tā : "he, him"; "she, her"

Plural forms:

> nǐmen : "you" (pl.)
>
> wǒmen : "we, us"
>
> tāmen : "they, them"

Note that "men" in Chinese is a suffix after personal pronouns indicating the plural form and is rarely used with other nouns. In the early stages of your study, use "men" only with personal pronouns.

2. nǐmen hǎo/nǐ hǎo

"Hǎo" means "good, fine." Both "nǐmen hǎo" and "nǐ hǎo" are greetings meaning "hello," "how do you do?" The only difference between them is that the former is a plural form that is used to greet more than one person, whereas the latter is commonly used in singular form.

3. xìng/jiào

"Xìng" in this chapter is used as a verb:

> Wǒ xìng Dīng.   (lit. = literally) I am surnamed Dīng.

"Jiào" here means "be called." One's full name, or one's given name, can be put after "jiào." The expression is:

> Wǒ jiào Dīng Yīměi.
>
> I am called Dīng Yīměi. (lit.)

4. shì

The main function of "shì" is the "be-verb" in Chinese, similar to "am, are, is" in English.

5. The possessive "de"

"De" after personal pronouns listed in note 1 or a specific person, place, or thing is used to express possession. For example:

> Dīng lǎoshī de xuésheng = teacher Ding's students*
>
> Wǒ de zhuānyè = my major

* Don't use "men" after "xuésheng" at the current stage. See note 1.

Note that the possessive "de" always precedes what it possesses.

6. lǎoshī

"Lǎoshī" means "teacher" and can stand alone or appear after a surname as a title.

7. Question words

In Chinese sentences, the position of a question word and the answer to the question is the same. In other words, you ask as you would be answered. Below is the list of the question words we will learn in this chapter:

shénme what	Nǐ You	xìng (are) surnamed		shénme? What?		(lit.)
	Wǒ I	xìng (am) surnamed		Dīng. Dīng.		(lit.)
nǎ which	Nǐ You	shì are	nǎ which	guó country	rén? person?	(lit.)
	Wǒ I	shì am		Zhōngguó Chinese	rén. person.	(lit.)

Please remember the grammar rule for question words. We will learn more question words in later chapters.

8. yě

"Yě" meaning "also" is a monosyllabic adverb that is usually placed directly after the subject and thus plays an important function in a sentence. It generally refers to the subject. For example:

Hànyǔ lǎoshī xìng Dīng. Wǒ yě xìng Dīng.
Chinese teacher is surnamed Dīng. I am surnamed Dīng too.

9. ma

In addition to question words, general questions in Chinese can be formed by adding the particle "ma" to the statements. There is no change in the word order of the sentence. The answer to a "ma" question is likely "yes" or "no." This is usually expressed by repeating the verb or adjective used in the questions. For example:

Question:	Nín shì Zhōngguó rén ma?	Are you Chinese?
Answer:	Shì,* wǒ shì Zhōngguó rén.	Yes, I'm Chinese. (positive)
	Bú shì, wǒ shì Yīngguó rén.	No, I'm British. (negative)

* "Shì" is also used like "yes" in English.

Question:	Nǐ xuéxí Hànyǔ ma?	Do you study Chinese?
Answer:	Wǒ xuéxí Hànyǔ.	I study Chinese. (positive)
	Wǒ bù xuéxí Hànyǔ.	I don't study Chinese. (negative)

10. shì de

Here, "de" has no meaning but softens the tone of a confirmation.

11. nǎ meaning "which" (see note 7)

12. Nǐ jiào shénme míngzi?

Here, "shénme" as a noun modifier is used to ask what kind of something is:

Question: Nǐ   jiào   shénme   míngzi?
            You   (are) called what   name?   (lit.)

"Shénme míngzi" is the question part, so, "míngzi" must be omitted in the answer to this question.

Answer: Wǒ jiào Wáng Èrmíng.

13. bù

"Bù," meaning "no, not," is placed before the word (a be-verb, adjective, adverb, and so on) negated. For example:

Question: Nǐ shì Yīngguó rén ma?
Answer: Bú shì, wǒ shì Měiguó rén.

14. tǐng······de

The adverbs "tǐng······de" (pretty, fairly), "hěn" (when it is stressed, it means "very"), "fēicháng" (extremely), and so on, are used to alter the strength of adjectives.

"Tǐng + adj. + de" can be regarded as a fixed pattern. The adjective is placed between "tǐng" and "de."

| tǐng nán de | pretty difficult |
| tǐng hǎo de | pretty good |

hěn adj. → If "hěn" is stressed, it means "very."

Wǒ de zhuānyè hěn nán.
My major is very difficult.

If "hěn" is not stressed, it does not mean "very." The above sentence means "My major is difficult." "Hěn" does not give emphasis to the strength of the adjective.

"fēicháng + adj." indicates a very high degree of the adjective.

| fēicháng nán | extremely difficult |
| fēicháng yǒu yìsi | extremely interesting |

Most commonly, there is NO "shì" between a subject and an adjective in Chinese. An adjective that is placed directly after a subject usually implies comparison with another thing.

Subject + adj.

For example:

Wǒ hǎo.	I'm better (than you).
Wǒ de zhuānyè nán.	My major is more difficult (than yours).
Wǒ de gōngzuò yǒu yìsi.	My job is more interesting (than yours).

If you just want to say "I'm fine," "My major is difficult," or "My job is interesting," you must put an unstressed "hěn" between the subject and the adjective.

Note that it is a big mistake to add the verb "to be" "shì" to these sentences.

If you want to express the different strength of the adjective, you can use "tǐng……de" or "fēicháng" or put stress on "hěn" before the adjective.

	English:	Subject	be-verb	adjective.	
		My major	is	difficult.	
	Chinese:	Subject	hěn (unstressed)	adjective.	
		Wǒ de zhuānyè	hěn	nán.	

	English:	Subject	be-verb	adverb	adjective.
1.		My major	is	pretty	difficult.
2.		My major	is	very	difficult.
3.		My major	Is	extremely	difficult.

	Chinese	Subject		adverb	adjective.	
1.		Wǒ de zhuānyè		tǐng	nán	de.
2.		Wǒ de zhuānyè		hěn	nán.	(stress hěn)
3.		Wǒ de zhuānyè		fēicháng	nán.	

15. ……ne?

"……ne?" question always follows a statement or topic. It means "And what about . . . ?" or "How about . . .?" For example,

Wǒ shì Yīngguó rén. Nǐ ne? I'm British. How about you?

Wǒ de zhuānyè tǐng nán de. Nǐ de zhuānyè ne?

My major is a bit challenging. How about yours?

16. Subj. + hěn + adj.

See note 14.

17. Subj. + fēicháng + adj.

See note 14.

18. zàijiàn "good-bye"

"Zài" is an adverb meaning "again, one more time." "Jiàn" is a verb meaning "see." "Zàijiàn" literally means "see you again someday."

Exercises

I. Listen to the following dialog and do the exercises.

1. Choose the correct answer.

   (1) Where is Teacher Dīng from?

   A. Měiguó   B. Yīngguó   C. Zhōngguó

   (2) Where is Wáng Èrmíng from?

   A. Měiguó   B. Yīngguó   C. Zhōngguó

   (3) What is Wáng Èrmíng's major?

   A. jīngjì   B. fǎlǜ   C. Zhōngguó

2. Decide whether the statements are true (T) or false (F).

   (1) Dīng lǎoshī bú shì Xiānggǎng rén. (   )

   (2) Wáng Èrmíng shì Yīngguó rén, tā xuéxí jīngjì zhuānyè. (   )

II. Choose the correct words and fill in the blanks.

xìng   jiào   shì   de   yě   ma   bù   tǐng

1. Nǐ shì Zhōngguó rén _____?
2. Wǒ shì Dīng lǎoshī _____ xuésheng.
3. Nǐhǎo, wǒ _____ Wáng, wǒ _____ Wáng Èrmíng.
4. Wǒ de gōngzuò _____ yǒu yìsi de.
5. A: Nǐ _____ Měiguó rén ma?

   B: _____, Wǒ shì Yīngguó rén.
6. A: Rènshi nǐ hěn gāoxìng.

   B: Rènshi nǐ wǒ _____ hěn gāoxìng.

III. Rearrange the words to form coherent sentences.

1. nǎ   guó   nǐ   rén   shì

   _____

2. bù (bú)   wǒ   shì   rén   Zhōngguó

   _____

3. jiào   shénme   nǐ   míngzi

   _____

4. tǐng   zhuānyè   wǒ de   de   nán

   _____

5. nǐmen   wǒ   shì   de   lǎoshī   Hànyǔ

   _____

IV. Complete the following dialog.

1. A: Nǐhǎo, nǐ xìng shénme?

    B: Wǒ xìng _____, jiào _____.

2. A: Nǐ shì nǎ guó rén?

    B: Wǒ shì _____ rén.

3. A: Nǐ xuéxí shénme zhuānyè?

    B: Wǒ xuéxí _____ zhuānyè.

4. A: Rènshi nǐ hěn gāoxìng.

    B: Rènshi nǐ _____.

V. Introduce yourself.

This is your first Chinese class. Please introduce yourself to your classmates in Chinese with the words given in the table.

| nǐ hǎo | xìng | jiào | rén | xuéxí | yǒu yìsi |
| tīng……de | rènshi | gāoxìng | | | |

Culture Note

The Chinese Language (Hanyu) and Chinese Names

The Chinese language (Hànyǔ), the major language of the Chinese people, with a history of more than 5,000 years, is one of the oldest languages in the world. Chinese belongs to the Sino-Tibetan language family. Of the 56 ethnic groups in China, the Han, Hui, and other ethnic groups, constituting 94% of the population of China, speak Chinese. Chinese includes variants from seven main dialect groups. Putonghua, literally "common speech," is based on the northern dialect, using the dialect of Beijing as the basis for its pronunciation and modern vernacular literature for grammatical structure.

The surnames of Chinese people appeared during matriarchal society, when clans were constituted with mothers at the center. Clans distinguished themselves from each other by using the name. In China, the surname comes first, followed by the given name. The latter has its own traditions and features. It can have one or two characters. Chinese names usually have a certain meaning, expressing some kind of wish. There are no exact statistics on how many surnames there are in China. Contemporary Chinese uses about 3,500 Chinese surnames. Of the 100 commonly used surnames, the three commonest are Li, Wang, and Zhang.

Ren Qiliang, ed., *Chinese Common Knowledge Series: Culture* (Hong Kong: Hong Kong China Tourism Press, 2005), 66–67.
Liu Xun, *New Practical Chinese Reader 1* (Beijing: Beijing Language and Culture University Press), 14.

第一课　认识你们很高兴

老师　　：你们好！

学生1 & 2：您好！

老师　　：我姓丁。我是你们的汉语老师。你姓什么？

学生1　　：我也姓丁，叫丁一美。我是您的学生。我学习法律专业。您是中国人吗？

老师　　：是的。你是哪国人？

学生1　　：我是英国人。（问学生2）你叫什么名字？

学生2　　：我叫王二明，也是丁老师的学生。

学生1　　：你是英国人吗？

学生2　　：不，我是美国人。

老师　　：你也学习法律吗？

学生2　　：不是，我学习经济。

老师　　：你的专业难吗？

学生2　　：我的专业挺难的。（问学生1）你的专业呢？

学生1　　：我的专业很难。丁老师，您的工作有意思吗？

老师　　：我的工作非常有意思。认识你们很高兴。

学生1 & 2：认识您我们也很高兴。再见。

老师　　：再见。

2
My family

Student 1 : Hello. Are you busy?
Student 2 : No, I'm not busy. Come in. Have a seat.
Student 1 : What's this?
Student 2 : It's a photo. (*Student 2 points to the photo.*) This is my family.
Student 1 : Who are these two people?
Student 2 : This is my dad. This is my mom.
Student 1 : Who's she?
Student 2 : She's my elder sister. She's pretty. How many family members do you have?

máng	忙	adj.	busy
qǐng	请		please
jìn	进	v.	to come in
zuò	坐	v.	to sit
zhè	这	pron.	this
zhāng	张	m.w.	piece; sheet
zhàopiàn	照片	n.	photo
tā	他	pron.	he; him
tāmen	他们	pron.	they
dōu	都	adv.	all; both

Dì-èr kè

Wǒ de jiārén

Xuésheng 1 : Nǐ hǎo! Nǐ máng ma?
Xuésheng 2 : Bù máng.[1] Qǐng[2] jìn, qǐng zuò.
Xuésheng 1 : Zhè[3] shì shénme?
Xuésheng 2 : Zhè shì yì[4] zhāng[5] zhàopiàn. (*zhǐ zhe zhàopiàn*). Tāmen dōu[6] shì wǒ de jiārén.
Xuésheng 1 : Zhè shì shéi?[7]
Xuésheng 2 : Zhè shì wǒ de bàba; zhè shì wǒ de māma.
Xuésheng 1 : Tā shì shéi?
Xuésheng 2 : Tā shì wǒ de jiějie. Tā hěn piàoliang. Nǐ jiā[8] yǒu[9] jǐ[10] kǒu[11] rén?

jiā	家	n.	family
jiārén	家人	n.	family member
shéi	谁	pron.	who; whom
bàba	爸爸	n.	father
māma	妈妈	n.	mother
tā	她	pron.	she; her
jiějie	姐姐	n.	elder sister
piàoliang	漂亮	adj.	pretty; beautiful
yǒu	有	v.	to have
jǐ	几		how many ...
kǒu	口	m.w.	measure word for the number of family members

Student 1 : One, two, three, four, five, six. There are six members in my family: my dad, my mom, my elder brother, my younger brother, my younger sister, and me.

Student 2 : Do you miss them?

Student 1 : I don't miss them. I miss my boyfriend, though, very much. How about your family?

Student 2 : I also have six family members. My dad, my mom, my elder sister, two younger sisters, and me. I don't have any brothers.

Student 1 : Your dorm is very big, and very beautiful.

Student 2 : Thank you. How's your dorm?

Student 1 : My dorm is also quite big. See, this is my dorm. (*Points at the photo in the cell phone.*)

Student 2 : What's that?

sān	三	num.	three
sì	四	num.	four
wǔ	五	num.	five
liù	六	num.	six
gēge	哥哥	n.	elder brother
dìdi	弟弟	n.	younger brother
mèimei	妹妹	n.	younger sister
hé	和	conj.	and
xiǎng	想	v.	to miss
nán	男	n.	man; male
nán péngyou	男朋友	n.	boyfriend

Xuésheng 1 : Yī, èr, sān, sì, wǔ, liù. Wǒ jiā yǒu liù kǒu rén. Bàba, māma, gēge, dìdi, mèimei hé[12] wǒ.
Xuésheng 2 : Nǐ xiǎng bu xiǎng[13] tāmen?
Xuésheng 1 : Wǒ bù xiǎng tāmen. Wǒ fēicháng xiǎng wǒ de nán péngyou. Nǐ jiā yǒu jǐ kǒu rén?
Xuésheng 2 : Wǒ jiā yě yǒu liù kǒu rén. Bàba, māma, jiějie, liǎng[14] ge mèimei hé wǒ. Wǒ méiyǒu gēge, yě méiyou dìdi.
Xuésheng 1 : Nǐ de sùshè hěn dà, yě hěn piàoliang.
Xuésheng 2 : Xièxie. Nǐ de sùshè zěnme yàng?[15]
Xuésheng 1 : Wǒ de sùshè yě tǐng dà de. Nǐ kàn, zhè shì wǒ de sùshè. (*Xuésheng 1 zhǐ zhe shǒujī li de zhàopiàn.*)
Xuésheng 2 : Nà[16] ge dōngxi shì shénme?

liǎng	两	num.	two (used before measure word; not used in counting number)
gè	个	m.w.	measure word for general use
méiyǒu	没有	v.	to not have
sùshè	宿舍	n.	dormitory
dà	大	adj.	big; large
xièxie	谢谢		thanks; thank you
zěnme yàng	怎么样	q.w.	how about
nǐ kàn	你看		Look!
nà	那	pron.	that
dōngxi	东西	n.	thing

Student 1 : That's a sock.

Student 2 : What's that red thing?

Student 1 : That's a small apple.

Student 2 : Your sock is on the table? The apple is on your sock?

Student 1 : Yes, as you can see, my cell phone and pen are on the pillow, and my Chinese book and bread are under the chair.

Student 2 : Although your dorm room is very big, it's very messy.

zhī	只	m.w.	one of a pair
wàzi	袜子	n.	socks
zài	在	v.	someone or something in/on/at someplace
zhuōzi	桌子	n.	table; desk
shàngbian	上边	n.	on; above
hóngsè	红色	n.	color red

Xuésheng 1 : Nà shì yì zhī[17] wàzi.

Xuésheng 2 : Nà ge hóngsè de[18] dōngxi ne?

Xuésheng 1 : Nà shì yí ge xiǎo píngguǒ.

Xuésheng 2 : Nǐ de wàzi zài[19] zhuōzi shàngbian?! Píngguǒ zài nǐ de wàzi shàngbian?!

Xuésheng 1 : Shì ya,[20] nǐ kàn, wǒ de shǒujī hé bǐ zài zhěntou shàngbian, Hànyǔ shū hé miànbāo zài yǐzi xiàbian.

Xuésheng 2 : Suīrán nǐ de sùshè hěn dà, dànshì[21] tài luàn le.[22]

shǒujī	手机	n.	cell phone
bǐ	笔	n.	pen
zhěntou	枕头	n.	pillow
shū	书	n.	book
miànbāo	面包	n.	bread
yǐzi	椅子	n.	chair
xiàbian	下边	n.	under; underneath
suīrán	虽然	conj.	although
dànshì	但是	conj.	but
tài……le	太……了		extremely; excessively
luàn	乱	adj.	messy

Grammar

1. bù máng

In Chapter 1, we discussed the use of "bù" and "hěn" to indicate negation. If you just want to say "I am not busy" in Chinese, "bù" is used to replace "hěn." The sentence is

> Wǒ bù máng.

"Hěn" can follow "bù," meaning "not very". For example:

> Wǒ bù hěn máng.
> I'm not very busy.

Note that "shì" cannot be used in an adjective-predicate sentence.

See note 13, Chapter 1.

2. qǐng

"Qǐng," meaning "please," must precede a verb in Chinese. As in:

| Come in, please. | Qǐng jìn. |
| Sit down, please. | Qǐng zuò. |

3. zhè, nà

There are two functions of the determinatives "zhè" (this or these) and "nà" (that or those).

Function 1: "zhè" or "nà" and "shì" can be bound together in Chinese. The expression "zhè shì" or "nà shì" can indicate either the singular or plural. For example:

> Zhè shì wǒ de xuésheng.
> This is my student.
> Or, these are my students.

Whether "xuésheng" is singular or plural depends on the context.

Function 2: a "zhè or nà + measure word" combination, such as "zhè ge" or "nà ge," can form a noun phrase, meaning "this one" or "that one." A noun or a noun phrase can follow a combination such as "zhè zhāng zhàopiàn" (this photo), or "nà ge dōngxi" (that thing).

4. Numbers

For the cardinal numbers zero to ten:

0	1	2	3	4	5	6	7	8	9	10
líng	yī	èr	sān	sì	wǔ	liù	qī	bā	jiǔ	shí

Numbers ranging from 11 to 99 are combinations of numbers 1 to 10. For example:

11	shíyī	10 and 1
12	shí'èr	10 and 2
13	shísān	10 and 3
...		
99	jiǔshíjiǔ	90 and 9

5. Measure word (hereafter abbreviated m.w.)

To say one photo, a family member, and so on, a measure word must be placed between the number and the noun. Many nouns require specific measure words. It is best to learn the measure word with the noun for which it is used. "Gè" is the most common measure word for individual things and persons, as in:

yí ge rén   one person.

In addition to "gè," there is a wide range of commonly used measure words. For example, "zhāng" is used before a noun implying a flat object such as a photo and paper, as in:

yì zhāng zhàopiàn   one (sheet of a) photo.

"Kǒu" always precedes "rén" and only measures the number of family members in the following sentences:

Nǐ jiā yǒu jǐ kǒu rén?   How many people are there in your family?
Wǒ jiā yǒu liù kǒu rén.   There are six people in my family.

"Gè" is rarely used in the above sentences.

"Zhī" is one of a pair.

The measure word "wàzi" (socks) should be "shuāng" (pair). In the text, "zhī" not "shuāng" is used because there is only one sock in the photo.

6. dōu

"Dōu" is an adverb when it precedes a verb, meaning "in all cases, all, both." Never place "dōu" before a noun.

7. shéi

"Shéi" is a question word meaning "who, whom." Review note 7, Chapter 1 for question words.

Nǐ shì shéi?   Who are you? (literally You are who?)
Zhè shì shéi?   Who is this person? (literally This person is who?)

8. nǐ jiā

"Nǐ jiā" comes from "nǐ de jiā." The particle "de" is dropped between a personal pronoun and words indicating relatives, friends, "jiā," and so on.

9. yǒu/méiyǒu

"Yǒu" means "have" or "there is (are)." For example:

> Wǒ jiā yǒu liù kǒu rén.

There are six people in my family. (lit. My family has six people.)

> Wǒ yǒu gēge.
> I have an elder brother.

Only "méi" can be used to negate "yǒu." Never use "bù." For example:

> Wǒ méiyǒu gēge.
> I don't have a brother.

10. jǐ

We will study a very important question word to ask the quantity of something. It is "jǐ," which implies that the number involved is below 10. It always requires a measure word. For example:

> Nǐ jiā yǒu jǐ kǒu rén?   How many people are there in your family?
> Nǐ yǒu jǐ ge dìdi?   How many younger brothers do you have?

Moreover, "jǐ" can be used in a question to ask the specific time, date, or day of the week. These functions will be discussed in Chapter 5.

11. kǒu

> See note 5.

12. hé

"Hé" means "and." It is used to connect nouns, noun phrases, and pronouns but rarely verbs, adjectives, or whole clauses:

> Tā xuéxí Hànyǔ hé fǎlǜ.
> He studies Chinese and law.

Whereas:

> Tā xuéxí Hànyǔ, wǒ xuéxí fǎlǜ.
> He studies Chinese, (and) I study law.

Inserting "hé" between the two clauses in the above sentence would be a big mistake in Chinese.

13. verb-not-verb/adj.-not-adj. questions

The patterns are also known as affirmative-negative questions. These take the form of an affirmative verb or adjective immediately followed by its negative; that is:

13.1 Question 1:

Subject	Verb-not-verb	Object?
Nǐ	xiǎng bu xiǎng	tāmen?

Do you miss them or not?

In question 1, the verb is "xiǎng." When your answer is positive, you need to say

"xiǎng."

The verb "xiǎng" in this case is the equivalent of "Yes." If the answer is negative, you need to say

Bù xiǎng.

The negative form "Bù xiǎng" in this case is the equivalent of "No."

13.2 Question 2:

Subject	adj.-not-adj.?
Nǐ de zhuānyè	nán bu nán?

Is your major difficult or not?

When your answer is positive, you need to say

Hěn nán.

If the answer is negative, you need to say

Bù nán.

The adjectives "Hěn nán" and "Bù nán" are respectively the equivalent of "Yes" and "No."

14. èr versus liǎng

In Chinese, both "èr" and "liǎng" mean two. However, their usage is different.

14.1 "Èr" is used when merely stating a number value such as 2, 12, and so on.

14.2 "Èr" is used as an ordinal number such as "èryuè," "February" (lit. the second month of the year).

14.3 "Liǎng" is used in front of measure words such as "liǎng ge mèimei," "two younger sisters."

14.4 "Gè" (or ge) is a common measure word. See note 5.

15. zěnme yàng

A question word, "zěnme yàng," meaning "how is . . . ," is placed after something or someone. It is used to ask for comments or opinions:

Nǐ de sùshè zěnme yàng?   What do you think of your dormitory?

16. nà: see note 3.

17. zhī: see note 5.

18. The modification "de"

"De" can be used as a particle of modification. It always precedes the noun it modifies.

19. Subject + zài + place word (p.w.).

19.1 "Zài" is a main verb, indicating someone or something is in/at/on someplace. So, a place word always follows "zài."

> Dīng lǎoshī zài sùshè.
> (Ms./Mr.) Dīng is in the dormitory.

Words indicating location can be any place name, such as "sùshè," or the name of a country. In this case, the localizer is optional.

If both the speaker and the listener know the place that is being discussed, the word denoting a place can be omitted. As in:

> Question: Dīng lǎoshī zài ma?
> Is Teacher Dīng (at the place)?
>
> Answer (positive): Tā zài.
> She is (at the place).
>
> Answer (negative): Tā bú zài.
> She is not (at the place).

Other place words such as "nǎr" (what place), "zhèr" (this place), and "nàr" (that place) will be discussed in Chapter 3.

19.2 A localizer can be attached to a noun or pronoun to form a place word. In the following sentence,

> Nǐ de wàzi zài zhuōzi shàngbian.
> Your sock is on the desk.

"Zhuōzi" is a noun, and "shàngbian" is a localizer. A noun-localizer combination is a place word in Chinese. The structures in Chinese and English are as follows:

Structure in English	Subject	is in/at/on	Noun/pronoun	
1.	Your sock	is	on the desk.	
2.	Chinese book	is	under the chair.	

Structure in Chinese	Subject	zài	Noun	Localizer
1.	Nǐ de wàzi	zài	zhuōzi	shàngbian.
2.	Hànyǔ shū	zài	yǐzi	xiàbian.

You will study more localizers "qiánbian" (front), "hòubian" (behind), "pángbiān" (side, beside), "lǐbian" (inside), and "wàibian" (outside) in Chapters 3 and 4.

20. shì ya "Yes/You're right."

In the text, the "shì ya" combination is used to affirm the speaker's observation "Your sock is on the desk and the apple is on your sock?" "Ya" is an interjection softening the tone of the sentence.

21. suīrán clause 1, dànshì clause 2

"Suīrán" (although) and "dànshì" (but) are always paired in Chinese. The structure is as follows:

Suīrán nǐ de sùshè hěn dà, dànshì tài luàn le.
Although your dormitory is big, it's too messy.

"Suīrán" can be placed after a subject in Chinese, and the meaning remains the same. For example:

Nǐ de sùshè suīrán hěn dà, dànshì tài luàn le.

Sometimes, "suīrán" can be omitted but "dànshì" cannot.

22. tài……le "very; too (excessively)"

It is important to remember that "tài……le" is a fixed sentence pattern. An adjective is always placed between "tài" and "le." When the adjective is positive, it sounds enthusiastic. When the adjective is negative, it always expresses disapproval. For example:

A positive example:

Zhōngguó tài piàoliang le!
China is extraordinarily beautiful!

A negative example:

Nǐ de sùshè tài luàn le!
Your dormitory is very messy!

In negative form, "le" is omitted and "bù" precedes "tài." The pattern is "bú tài adj." (not too adj.). For example:

Wǒ de zhuānyè bú tài nán.
My major is not too challenging.

Exercises

I. Listen to the following dialog and do the exercises.

1. Choose the correct answer.

    (1) How many members are there in Ding Yimei's family?

    A. wǔ kǒu   B. liù kǒu   C. qī kǒu

    (2) How many elder brothers does Ding Yimei have?

    A. yí ge   B. liǎng ge   C. sān ge

    (3) Where is Ding Yimei from?

    A. Yīngguó   B. Měiguó   C. Zhōngguó

2. Decide whether the statements are true (T) or false (F).

    (1) Dīng Yīměi de māma hé bàba shì lǎoshī. (   )

    (2) Dīng Yīměi de nán péngyou bú shì Měiguó rén; tā shì Yīngguó rén. (   )

II. Choose the correct words and fill in the blanks.

kǒu   zhāng   méi   zhè   jǐ   hé   liǎng   zài

1. Zhè shì yì _____ zhàopiàn.
2. Wàzi _____ zhuōzi shàngbian.
3. Wǒ jiā yǒu wǔ _____ rén, bàba, māma, _____ gè mèimei _____ wǒ.
4. _____ shì wǒ de nán péngyou, tā shì Měiguó rén.
5. A: Nǐ yǒu _____ ge gēge?

    B: Wǒ _____ yǒu gēge.

III. Make the sentences with the words given.

1. shéi   zhè   shì
2. wǒ de   tāmen   jiārén   shì   dōu
3. jiào   shénme   nǐ   míngzi
4. bù   xiǎng   jiārén   xiǎng   nǐ   nǐde
5. píngguǒ   wàzi   zhuōzi   zài   hé   xiàbian

IV. Use the following words to describe your room.

zài   shàngbian   xiàbian   píngguǒ   Hànyǔ shū   wàzi
zhuōzi   shǒujī   zhěntou   miànbāo   yǐzi   bǐ

V. Write a short paragraph to introduce your family members.

Culture Note

Earliest Ancestor of the Chinese Nation

Huangdi (Yellow Emperor) and Yandi (Red Emperor)

Huangdi and Yandi are the common ancestors of the Chinese nation, and Chinese people at home and abroad all call themselves "descendants of Yandi and Huangdi." As recorded in legends and ancient books, Huangdi was the first emperor in Chinese history. His surname was Ji. Yandi was also a legendary ruler, whose surname was Jiang.

Huangdi and Yandi both lived in the late period of China's primitive society about 4,000 years ago and were the leaders of two different tribes living along the Yellow River in present-day Shaanxi Province. Later, they expanded their territories along both sides of the Yellow River to the east. The Yandi had invaded the territory of another tribe, the Jiuli, whose leader was Chiyou. After the defeat, some people of the Jiuli fled to the south, while others were assimilated into the Yandi or Huangdi tribes.

Later, segments of the three tribes (Huangdi, Yandi, and Jiuli) settled in the Yellow River valley, where they began to develop China's ancient culture and eventually formed the mainstay of what we know today as the Chinese people. It is from this time that people began to call themselves "the descendants of Yandi and Huangdi."

Ren Qiliang, ed., *Chinese Common Knowledge Series—Culture* (Hong Kong: Hong Kong China Tourism Press, 2005), 5–6.

第二课　我的家人

学生1：你好！你忙吗？

学生2：不忙。请进，请坐。

学生1：这是什么？

学生2：这是一张照片。（指着照片）他们都是我的家人。

学生1：这是谁？

学生2：这是我的爸爸，这是我的妈妈。

学生1：她是谁？

学生2：她是我的姐姐。她很漂亮。你家有几口人？

学生1：一、二、三、四、五、六。我家有六口人。爸爸、妈妈、哥哥、弟弟、妹妹和我。

学生2：你想不想他们？

学生1：我不想他们。我非常想我的男朋友。你家有几口人？

学生2：我家也有六口人。爸爸、妈妈、姐姐、两个妹妹和我。我没有哥哥，也没有弟弟。

学生1：你的宿舍很大，也很漂亮。

学生2：谢谢。你的宿舍怎么样？

学生1：我的宿舍也挺大的。你看，这是我的宿舍。（指着手机里的照片）

学生2：那个东西是什么？

学生1：那是一只袜子。

学生2：那个红色的东西呢？

学生1：那是一个小苹果。

学生2：你的袜子在桌子上边？！苹果在你的袜子上边？！

学生1：是呀，你看，我的手机和笔在枕头上边，汉语书和面包在椅子下边。

学生2：虽然你的宿舍很大，但是太乱了……

3
Shopping

Sales clerk : Hello!
Student   : Hello! Is the phone card here expensive?
Sales clerk : The phone cards we sell here aren't expensive. They're very cheap.
Student   : How much is this cell phone card?
Sales clerk : Seventy-eight dollars.
Student   : Okay, I'd like to buy this phone card. I also want a loaf of bread, two bottles of beer, and a magazine.

zhèr	这儿	pron.	here; this place
diànhuà kǎ	电话卡	n.	phone card
kǎ	卡	n.	card
guì	贵	adj.	expensive
piányi	便宜	adj.	cheap
duōshao qián	多少钱	q.w.	how much (money) . . . ?
qián	钱	n.	money
qī	七	num.	seven
shí	十	num.	ten
bā	八	num.	eight

Dì-sān kè

Mǎi dōngxi

Diànyuán : Nǐ hǎo!
Xuésheng : Nǐ hǎo! Nǐmen zhèr[1] de diànhuàkǎ guì bu guì?
Diànyuán : Wǒmen zhèr de diànhuàkǎ bú guì, hěn piányi.
Xuésheng : Zhè zhāng diànhuàkǎ duōshao qián?[2]
Diànyuán : Qīshíbā kuài qián.[3]
Xuésheng : Hǎo de. Wǒ mǎi zhè zhāng diànhuàkǎ. Wǒ hái[4] xiǎng[5] mǎi yí ge miànbāo, liǎng píng píjiǔ hé yì běn zázhì.

kuài	块	m.w.	dollar
hǎo de	好的		alright; good
mǎi	买	v.	to buy
hái	还	adv.	additionally
xiǎng	想	v.	would like to; to want
píng	瓶	m.w.	bottle
píjiǔ	啤酒	n.	beer
běn	本	m.w.	
zázhì	杂志	n.	magazine

Sales clerk : That'll be one hundred nine dollars and fifty cents. Are you paying cash or by credit card?
Student   : I'll pay by Octopus card. May I ask how to get to Hong Kong U?
Sales clerk : You can take bus No. 23 or go by MTR.

yígòng	一共	adv.	altogether
bǎi	百	num.	hundred
líng	零	num.	zero
jiǔ	九	num.	nine
máo	毛	m.w.	ten cents
yòng	用	v.	to use
xiànjīn	现金	n.	cash
háishi	还是	q.w.	or
xìnyòng kǎ	信用卡	n.	credit card
Bādátōng	八达通	n.	Octopus card

Diànyuán: Yígòng[6] yìbǎi[7] líng jiǔ kuài wǔ máo. Nǐ yòng[8] xiànjīn háishi[9] xìnyòngkǎ?
Xuésheng: Wǒ yòng Bādátōng. Qǐngwèn,[10] zěnme qù[11] Xiānggǎng Dàxué?
Diànyuán: Nǐ zuò[12] èrshísān hào bāshì huòzhě[13] dìtiě ba.[14]

qǐngwèn	请问		may I ask . . .
wèn	问	v.	to ask
zěnme	怎么	q.w.	how (to)
qù	去	v.	to go
Xiānggǎng Dàxué	香港大学	n.	the University of Hong Kong
zuò	坐	v.	to sit; to take the bus/subway, etc.
hào	号	n.	number
bāshì	巴士	n.	bus
huòzhě	或者		or (used in a statement)
dìtiě	地铁	n.	subway
ba	吧	part.	a sentence particle indicating a suggestion

Student : Where's the bus stop and the MTR station? Is it far?

Sales clerk : They're very close. The MTR station is next to the 7-Eleven. The bus stop is in front of the 7-Eleven and the MTR station.

Student : Got it. The MTR station is behind the bus stop. Thank you. Good-bye.

Sales clerk : You're welcome. Good-bye.

Xuésheng: Bāshì zhàn hé dìtiě zhàn zài nǎr?[15] Yuǎn bu yuǎn?

Diànyuán: Hěn jìn, dìtiě zhàn zài Qī-shíyī pángbiān.[16] Bāshì zhàn zài Qī-shíyī hé dìtiě zhàn qiánbian.

Xuésheng: Míngbai le.[17] Dìtiě zhàn zài bāshì zhàn hòubian. Xièxie. Zàijiàn.

Diànyuán: Bú kèqi. Zàijiàn.

zhàn	站	n.	station
nǎr	哪儿	q.w.	where
yuǎn	远	adj.	far
jìn	近	adj.	near
Qī-shíyī	七十一 (7-11)	n.	7-Eleven
pángbiān	旁边	n.	beside
qiánbian	前边	n.	front
míngbai le	明白了		Got it! I see.
hòubian	后边	n.	behind
bú kèqi	不客气		You're welcome. Not at all.

Grammar

1. zhèr, nàr, and nǎr

We have discussed some place words and localizers in previous chapters. Now, we will study three more place words. They are:

"zhèr" (this place), used to indicate that the place is near the speaker; and

"nàr" (that place), used to indicate that the place is away from the speaker.

When they are used as localizers, "zhèr" and "nàr" can also combine with another noun or personal pronoun to make a place word. For example, "zhèr" and "nàr" can be put after "wǒ," but the combinations indicate "here by me" or "there by me" respectively. "Wǒ zhèr" is always used when the speaker is in his or her place, whereas "wǒ nàr" is always used when the speaker is at a distance from his or her place.

"Nǎr" (where) is a question word. It is used to ask for the location of something or someone. For example:

Dīng lǎoshī zài nǎr?

Where is Teacher Dīng?

It can also be placed directly after a geographical name, a noun, or a personal pronoun and means "which part of . . . , which place of . . ." As in:

Nǐ zài Zhōngguó nǎr xuéxí Hànyǔ?

In which city of China do you study Chinese?

Nǐ nǎr bù shūfu?

Where do you feel uncomfortable?

Review note 8, Chapter 1 for more information about the features of the question words.

2. duōshao qián? "How much (money) . . .?"

This is a question to ask "how much money." For example:

Zhè zhāng diànhuà kǎ duōshao qián?

How much is this phone card?

Do not add the verb "to be" "shì" to this question.

3. Money expressions

There are two ways to express money in Chinese. When we issue a contract, a check, or other paper document, we use the terms "yuán" (dollar), "jiǎo" (10 cents), and "fēn" (cent). Hence, RMB¥10.55 in Chinese is written:

shí yuán wǔ jiǎo wǔ fēn

In this chapter, we will study the terms "kuài" (dollar), "máo" (10 cents), and "fēn" (cent) that are used in spoken form. For example:

10.00	shí kuài (qián)
0.50	wǔ máo (qián)
0.05	wǔ fēn (qián)
10.55	shí kuài wǔ máo wǔ (fēn) (qián)

Note that:

3.1 "Qián" is usually omitted when it is at the end of a string. "Kuài" in a "number + kuài" combination can mean either "number + dollars" or "number + cubes/pieces" if it lacks a context. In order to prevent any confusion this may cause, it is safe to keep "qián" at the end of a string.

3.2 "Máo" or "fēn" is often omitted if it is the last item in a string. As in:

10.50	shí kuài wǔ (máo)
10.55	shí kuài wǔ máo wǔ (fēn)

3.3 When a zero appears in the number of "máo," which is in the middle of a string, "líng" must be used in spoken Chinese to replace the "number + máo" combination. For example:

10.05	shí kuài líng wǔ (fēn)

3.4 In general, "èr" should be changed to "liǎng" when the number precedes a measure word. However, "èr" must be used before a measure word if it is the last part of a larger number. For example:

12.55	shíèr kuài wǔ máo wǔ
62.00	liùshíèr kuài

3.5 "Fēn" cannot go higher than "9 fēn." You cannot say "25 fēn." You have to say:

0.25	liǎng máo wǔ (fēn)

Memorize the expressions below:

10 cents	20 cents	30 cents	40 cents	50 cents	60 cents	70 cents	80 cents	90 cents
yì máo	liǎng máo	sān máo	sì máo	wǔ máo	liù máo	qī máo	bā máo	jiǔ máo

3.6 In summary:

Spoken style	kuài	máo	fēn
0.35	nothing	sān	wǔ
1.05	yī	líng	wǔ
2.80	liǎng	bā	zero
12.25	shíèr	liǎng	wǔ
Written style	yuán	jiǎo	fēn

4. hái "additionally"

"Hái," meaning "additionally, in addition," is an adverb that refers to the action follows and the object of the verb:

> Wǒ mǎi yì zhāng diànhuàkǎ. Hái xiǎng mǎi yí ge miànbāo.
> I'll buy a phone card. In addition, I'd like to buy a bun.

5. xiǎng

"Xiǎng" can be used before another verb as a modal verb. It means "would like," as in:

Wǒ xiǎng mǎi yì píng píjiǔ.	I'd like to buy a bottle of beer.
Nǐ xiǎng bu xiǎng mǎi zázhì?	Would you like to buy a magazine?
Wǒ bù xiǎng xuéxí fǎlǜ.	I don't want to study law.

6. yígòng "all together; in all"

> Yígòng yìbǎi líng jiǔ kuài wǔ máo.
> (These things) all together (need) one hundred and nine dollars and fifty cents.

The present sentence is with a predicate only.

"Yígòng," an adverb, preceding a "verb + number + m.w. (+ noun)" combination, means the total number of the noun.

7. bǎi "hundred"

From 100 to 999, there are two important groups of numbers you need to remember:

7.1 If there is zero between the numbers, you must say "líng," as follows:

101	102	103	104	105
yìbǎi líng yī	yìbǎi líng èr	yìbǎi líng sān	yìbǎi líng sì	yìbǎi líng wǔ
106	107	108	109	
yìbǎi líng liù	yìbǎi líng qī	yìbǎi líng bā	yìbǎi líng jiǔ	

7.2 If one of the numbers from 11 to 19 comes to a large number above 100, "yī" must be pronounced before "shí." For example:

110	111	112	113	114
yìbǎi yīshí	yìbǎi yīshíyī	yìbǎi yīshíèr	yìbǎi yīshísān	yìbǎi yīshísì
115	116	117	118	119
yìbǎi yīshíwǔ	yìbǎi yīshíliù	yìbǎi yīshíqī	yìbǎi yīshíbā	yìbǎi yīshíjiǔ

Literally, the expression is "one hundred one ten," "one hundred one ten and one," and so on.

Note that the tones of "yī" are different when it occurs in a different digit of the higher numbers listed above. For the tone sandhi rules, see the Introduction.

8. yòng

One of the functions of "yòng" in Chinese is acting as a verb. It means "use." "Búyòng" (not use) is the negative form. For example:

Wǒ yòng xìnyòng kǎ.
I'll use a credit card (to buy it).

Wǒ búyòng diànhuà kǎ.
I don't use a phone card (to make calls).

Wǒ yòng xìnyòng kǎ mǎi diànhuà kǎ.
I use a credit card to purchase a phone card.

9. háishi (a choice question particle)

"Háishi" (or) is used only when asking someone to choose between alternatives. Note that these two alternatives must be of similar grammatical structure. For example:

9.1 Two nouns:

Nǐ shì lǎoshī háishi xuésheng?
Are you a teacher, or a student?

9.2 Two verbal phrases:

Nǐ xiǎng chī sānwénzhì háishi hē kāfēi?
Would you like to eat a sandwich, or drink coffee? (See Chapter 4.)

10. Qǐngwèn,……?

"Qǐngwèn" is used to call someone's attention to your question in a polite way. A question must follow. "Qǐngwèn" means "May (I) ask . . . ?"

11. zěnme + verb

"Zěnme," a question word, is used to ask "in what way or manner" to do something, following the pattern "how to (verb) something." For example:

Wǒ zěnme qù Xiānggǎng Dàxué?
How do I get to the University of Hong Kong?

Zěnme yòng shǒujī?
(Can you tell me) How to use a cell phone?

12. zuò

"Zuò" (originally means "sit"; see Chapter 2), which is used before a transportation vehicle such as a bus, subway, and so on, means "take the bus, subway" in Chinese.

13. huòzhě "or"

"Huòzhě" (or) is used in statements expressing the alternatives. Note that "háishi" is usually used in questions to ask for alternatives.

14. Suggestion + ba

When the particle "ba" follows a suggestion, it means "let's . . ." or "you could do something." We use the particle "ba" to soften the tone of a sentence. For example:

Nǐ zuò bāshì huòzhě dìtiě ba?	How about taking the bus or subway?
Mǎi píjiǔ ba!	Let's buy some beer.

15. nǎr "where"

See note 1.

16. pángbiān, qiánbian, and hòubian (localizers) (see note 19, Chapter 2)

17. míngbai le

"Le" is one of the important sentence particles in Chinese. Here, you will learn its first function, which indicates a new situation. "Míngbai le" indicates that the speaker's situation has transformed from "not clear or not understand" to "clear or understand."

Exercises

I. Listen to the following dialogs and fill in the blanks.

1. A: Nǐhǎo. Qǐngwèn, yì zhāng diànhuà kǎ duōshao qián?

   B: Wǒmen zhèr de diànhuà kǎ hěn _____, yì zhāng _____ kuài qián.

   A: Hǎo de, wǒ mǎi yì zhāng diànhuà kǎ. Qǐngwèn, zhèr yǒu píjiǔ ma? Yì píng píjiǔ duōshao qián?

   B: Yì píng píjiǔ _____ kuài qián, liǎng píng píjiǔ _____ kuài qián.

   A: Hǎo de, wǒ mǎi _____ píng píjiǔ.

   B: Yì zhāng diànhuà kǎ hé _____ píng píjiǔ, yígòng _____ kuài qián, nǐ yòng xiànjīn háishi _____?

   A: Wǒ yòng _____.

2. A: Nǐhǎo. _____, zěnme qù Xiānggǎng Dàxué?

   B: Nǐ _____ bāshì háishi dìtiě?

   A: Bāshì zhàn jìn háishi dìtiě zhàn jìn?

   B: Dìtiě zhàn hěn jìn, zài 7-Eleven _____. Bāshì zhàn hěn _____.

   A: Hǎo de, wǒ zuò dìtiě, _____, zàijiàn.

   B: Bú kèqi, zàijiàn.

II. Choose the correct words and fill in the blanks. Each word can be used only once.

gè   zhāng   kǒu   píng   běn   zhī   kuài

1. Zhè shì yì _____ wàzi.
2. A: Wǒ mǎi yì _____ diànhuà kǎ, sān _____ zázhì, sì _____ píjiǔ, yígòng duōshao qián?

   B: Yígòng yìbǎi líng liù _____.
3. Wǒ jiā yǒu sì _____ rén.
4. Nà shì yí _____ xiǎo píngguǒ.

III. Write sentences with the words given.

1. nǎr
2. huòzhě
3. zěnme + verb
4. hái
5. zài……pángbiān

IV. Ask questions about the information underlined.

1. A: Yì zhāng diànhuà kǎ <u>èrshíwǔ kuài</u>.
   B: _____?

2. A: Dìtiě zhàn zài <u>7-11 pángbiān</u>.
   B: _____?

3. A: Wǒ mǎi <u>yí ge miànbāo hé liǎng píng píjiǔ</u>.
   B: _____?

4. A: Wǒ jiā yǒu <u>sì</u> kǒu rén.
   B: _____?

V. Role-play

Suppose you are at a food market in Hong Kong and you want to buy something for your dinner. Write a dialog with the words you have learned.

Salesperson: _____

Customer: _____

Salesperson: _____

Customer: _____

Salesperson: _____

Customer: _____

Salesperson: _____

Customer: _____

Culture Note

Travelling in Hong Kong

Hong Kong's culture is a melting pot of customs and traditions, influenced by thousands of years of immigration. Hong Kong culture is underpinned by the Cantonese dialect and people. A remarkable history that moves through Chinese immigration, colonization by the British and subsequent handover into a Special Administrative Region of China, it should come as no surprise that Hong Kong is such a melting pot of Eastern and Western characteristics.

Hong Kong offers the quintessential shopping experience: from its giant designer malls and packed street markets to its bargain outlets, you'll find a product with your name on it. But the city is also home to a number of celebrated fashion designers, stand-alone boutiques, and quirky shopping malls often tucked away out of sight.

Hong Kong comes alive at night, abuzz with diners, revelers, theatergoers, and even market traders still out plying their wares. The nightlife scene is rightly legendary: there is something to do at every time of the day in this city that never sleeps. You can spend a whole night in Lan Kwai Fong and Wan Chai, as these two places are the most renowned night owl destinations.

Hong Kong is one of the most talked-about dining destinations in the world: it's where celebrity chefs from across the globe compete to showcase their talent—and where diners come in droves to be the first to tuck in. But as densely packed as this city is with Michelin-starred restaurants and venues you'll queue all night for, it also excels in something you'll struggle to find anywhere else in the world—rich, local gems steeped in tradition, and humble, neighborhood family favorites.

Hong Kong Tourism Board Website, accessed October 28, 2016, http://www.discoverhongkong.com/eng/index.jsp.

第三课　买东西

店员：你好！

学生：你好！你们这儿的电话卡贵不贵？

店员：我们这儿的电话卡不贵，很便宜。

学生：这张电话卡多少钱？

店员：七十八块钱。

学生：好的，我买这张电话卡。我还想买一个面包、两瓶啤酒和一本杂志。

店员：一共一百零九块五毛。你用现金还是信用卡？

学生：我用八达通。请问，怎么去香港大学？

店员：你坐23号巴士或者地铁吧。

学生：巴士站和地铁站在哪儿？远不远？

店员：很近，地铁站在7-11旁边，巴士站在7-11和地铁站前边。

学生：明白了。地铁站在巴士站后边。谢谢。再见。

店员：不客气。再见。

4
Where to eat

Student 1 : Where do you usually eat?

Student 2 : I often go to the student canteen beside Starbucks to have a meal. Let's go there for a meal today!

Student 1 : Is the food in that student canteen any good?

Student 2 : It's quite good. The qie*-dan sandwich is tasty.

Student 1 : A sandwich made of eggplant? That's a little weird.

Student 2 : No. It's not eggplant. It's tomato.

Student 1 : Wow . . .

Student 2 : The beef rice noodles and dumpling noodles there aren't so good, but they're very cheap.

* Qie is the abbreviation of tomato or eggplant in Chinese.

chángcháng	常常	adv.	often
chī fàn	吃饭	v.	to eat a meal
Xīngbākè	星巴克	n.	Starbucks
cāntīng	餐厅	n.	canteen
jīntiān	今天	n.	today
nàr	那儿	pron.	there; that place
hǎo chī	好吃	adj.	delicious; tasty
qié-dàn sānwénzhì	茄蛋三文治	n.	tomato-egg sandwich
qiézi	茄子	n.	eggplant

Dì-sì kè

Qù nǎr chī fàn

Xuésheng 1 : Nǐ chángcháng[1] qù nǎr chī fàn?[2]

Xuésheng 2 : Wǒ chángcháng qù Xīngbākè pángbiān de xuésheng cāntīng[3] chī fàn. Wǒmen jīntiān[4] qù nàr chī ba!

Xuésheng 1 : Nà ge xuésheng cāntīng de dōngxi hǎo chī[5] ma?

Xuésheng 2 : Tǐng hǎo chī de. Nàr de qié-dàn sānwénzhì hěn hǎo chī.

Xuésheng 1 : Yòng qiézi zuò[6] sānwénzhì? Tài qíguài le! Tài nán chī le!

Xuésheng 2 : Bú shì. Nà shì fānqié. Bú shì qiézi.

Xuésheng 1 : Ò[7]. . .

Xuésheng 2 : Nàr de niúròu héfěn hé yúntūn miàn suīrán bù hǎo chī, dànshì hěn piányi.

zuò	做	v.	to make; to do
qíguài	奇怪	adj.	weird; odd; strange
nán chī	难吃	adj.	taste awful
fānqié	番茄	n.	tomato
ò	哦	inter.	
niúròu	牛肉	n.	beef
héfěn	河粉	n.	rice noodle
yúntūn	云吞	n.	wonton
miàn	面	n.	noodle

Student 1 : I don't like the canteens on the campus, so I often go to eat at the restaurants outside campus.
Student 2 : Which restaurants? Are they expensive?
Student 1 : The restaurant behind the bus station is very good. The iced milk-tea and hot coffee are both very tasty and very cheap.
Student 2 : Great. Let's have dinner there tonight. I want to have the iced milk-tea.
Student 1 : If we eat there, we have to use chopsticks. Do you know how to use chopsticks?

Xuésheng 1 : Wǒ bù xǐhuan dàxué lǐbian de cāntīng. Wǒ chángcháng qù dàxué wàibian[8] de cāntīng.

Xuésheng 2 : Nǎ ge cāntīng? Guì bu guì?

Xuésheng 1 : Bāshì zhàn hòubian de cāntīng hěn hǎo. Nàr de bīng nǎichá hé rè kāfēi[9] dōu hěn hǎo hē, yě hěn piányi.

Xuésheng 2 : Tài hǎo le, wǒmen jīntiān wǎnshang qù nàr chī fàn ba. Wǒ xiǎng hē bīng nǎichá.

Xuésheng 1 : Zài nàr chī fàn de huà, wǒmen jiù[10] děi[11] yòng kuàizi. Nǐ huì[12] yòng kuàizi ma?

xǐhuan	喜欢	v.	to like; to enjoy
lǐbian	里边	n.	inside
wàibian	外边	n.	outside
bīng	冰	n./adj.	ice; iced
nǎichá	奶茶	n.	milk tea
rè	热	adj.	hot
kāfēi	咖啡	n.	coffee
hǎo hē	好喝	adj.	(drink, soup) tastes good
tài hǎo le	太好了		Great! Wonderful!
wǎnshang	晚上	n.	evening; night
……de huà, jiù……	……的话，就……	conj.	If . . . then . . . (condition)
děi	得		have to; must
kuàizi	筷子	n.	chopsticks
huì	会	v.	know how to do something

Student 2 : Oh . . . I don't know how to use chopsticks. Don't they have knives and forks?
Student 1 : No, so you should learn how to eat with chopsticks.
Student 2 : Can you teach me?
Student 1 : If you pay for my dinner today, I will.
Student 2 : You're so bad . . .

Xuésheng 2: Ò……bú tài huì. Tāmen nàr yǒu méiyou dāo chā?

Xuésheng 1: Méiyou. Nǐ yīnggāi[13] xuéxí yòng kuàizi chī fàn.

Xuésheng 2: Nǐ jiāo wǒ, hǎo ma?[14]

Xuésheng 1: Nǐ jīntiān wǎnshang qǐng[15] wǒ chī fàn de huà, wǒ jiù jiāo nǐ.

Xuésheng 2: Nǐ tài huài le[16]……

dāo	刀	n.	knife
chā	叉	n.	fork
yīnggāi	应该	v.	should; ought to
jiāo	教	v.	to teach
hǎo ma	好吗		a sentence particle indicate a suggestion
qǐng	请	v.	to treat somebody to a meal, etc.
huài	坏	adj.	bad

Grammar

1. chángcháng and bù cháng

"Chángcháng," meaning "often," is an adverb preceding the main verb in the sentence. Sometimes, "cháng" is used instead of "chángcháng." In the negative form, we never say "bù chángcháng" but "bù cháng."

2. A sentence with verbal constructions in a series in Chinese

A sentence in which two or more verbs or verbal constructions are used as the predicate of the same subject is called a sentence with verbal constructions in a series. For example:

Subject	adv.	verb phrase 1	verb phrase 2
Nǐ	chángcháng	qù nǎr	chī fàn?

3. Xīngbākè pángbiān de xuésheng cāntīng

"Xīngbākè pángbiān" (beside Starbucks) is a place word consisting of a place and a localizer. The whole combination before "de" is a modifier that is used to modify the noun "xuésheng cāntīng" (student canteen). The phrase emphasizes that the "student canteen" is not any other one but the one that is next to Starbucks.

4. Time words

Time words are very important in Chinese because they can tell the tense of the actions. "Tiān" is similar to a suffix that can form the names of the days.

qiántiān	zuótiān	jīntiān	míngtiān	hòutiān
the day before yesterday	yesterday	today	tomorrow	the day after tomorrow

For example:

Wǒ zuótiān bù máng, jīntiān hěn máng, míngtiān fēicháng máng.
I was not busy yesterday. I'm busy today and will be extremely busy tomorrow.

In addition to the names of the days are the terms "zǎoshang," "shàngwǔ," "zhōngwǔ," "xiàwǔ," "wǎnshang" indicating "early morning," "morning," "noon," "afternoon," and "evening and night" respectively in Chinese. These five terms expressing the different parts of a day are similar to a.m. and p.m. when preceding time points in Chinese. They will be discussed in Chapter 5.

If there are several time words in a series, the order should descend from larger to smaller units. For example:

Name of day	Part of day	Time point
jīntiān	shàngwǔ	9:00 a.m.
míngtiān	zhōngwǔ	12:30 p.m.

More time words including time points will be discussed in Chapter 5.

5. hǎo chī/nánchī

Sometimes, "hǎo + verb" and "nán + verb" is a pair of words with opposite meanings. They are compounded with different verbs and have different meanings. There are two groups as follows:

5.1 "hǎo" (good) vs. "nán" (bad)

hǎo chī: good to eat, tasty	vs.	nánchī: taste bad
hǎo hē: good to drink	vs.	nánhē: (drinks) taste bad
hǎokàn: good-looking	vs.	nánkàn: ugly-looking

5.2 "hǎo" (easy) vs. "nán" (difficult)

hǎo xué: easy to learn	vs.	nán xué: hard to learn
hǎo zuò: easy to do	vs.	nán zuò: hard to do
hǎo mǎi: easy to buy	vs.	nán mǎi: hard to buy

Note that all the above terms can follow tǐng, hěn, tài, or fēicháng.

6. zuò

There are different meanings and functions of "zuò." It means "to do," "to make," "to behave," and so on. As in:

yòng qiézi zuò sānwénzhì	use eggplant to make a sandwich
Nǐ zuò shénme gōngzuò?	What do you do?
zuò hǎorén	behave like a good person

7. ò

"Ò" is an interjection indicating that the speaker is clear about something. For example:

A: Rè kāfēi 25 kuài, bīng kāfēi 20 kuài.

A: Hot coffee is 25 dollars and iced coffee is 20 dollars.

B: Ò. Wǒ yào rè kāfēi.

B: Sure. I want (some) hot coffee.

8. "Lǐbian" means "inside" and "wàibian" means "outside."

9. bīng and rè

"Bīng" is a noun meaning "ice." When it precedes another noun, such as a drink, it means "iced," as in:

bīng nǎichá	iced milk tea
bīng shuǐ	ice water

"Rè" is an adjective meaning "hot." It can be used to describe weather or can be followed by a drink, such as:

| rè kāfēi | hot coffee |
| rè shuǐ | hot water |

Note that "dòng" meaning "freezing, cold" is used to replace "bīng" in Hong Kong. For example:

| dòng nǎichá | iced milk tea |
| dòng kāfēi | iced coffee |

10. Condition + de huà, (subj.) + jiù + result.

An English conditional sentence uses "if" at the beginning of a conditional clause, whereas in Chinese the particle ". . . de huà" is used at the end of the first clause to indicate a condition. "Jiù……" must follow the subject in the result clause in Chinese. Compare the following sentences:

Nǐ chī de huà, wǒ jiù chī.
If you eat (it), I will eat (it).

Nǐ xuéxí Hànyǔ de huà, wǒ jiù xuéxí Hànyǔ.
If you study Chinese, I will study Chinese.

11. děi

"Děi" is an auxiliary verb meaning "must, have to." An auxiliary verb comes before the main verb and helps it. Note that the negative form "don't have to" in Chinese is "bú yòng" NOT "bù děi."

12. huì "know how to"

"Huì" is another auxiliary verb meaning "know how to," such as:

| Wǒ huì yòng kuàizi. | I know how to use chopsticks. |
| Wǒ bú huì zuò sānwénzhì. | I don't know how to make a sandwich. |

"Huì" can also be a main verb when speaking about knowledge of a language:

| Wǒ huì Hànyǔ. | I know the Chinese language. |
| Wǒ bú huì Hànyǔ. | I don't know the Chinese language. |

13. yīnggāi

"Yīnggāi," meaning "should, ought to," is another common auxiliary verb. For example:

| Nǐ yīnggāi xuéxí Hànyǔ. | You should study Chinese. |
| Nǐ bù yīnggāi hē píjiǔ. | You shouldn't drink beer. |

14. hǎo ma? (suggestion)

"Hǎo ma" can follow statements and make suggestions about future actions or activities. When the suggestion is "let's . . . ," "suggestion ba" and "suggestion, hǎo ma?" are similar. In this case, the latter is more polite, and it expects more ideas/opinions from the listener. Compare the following two sentences:

Wǒmen qù xuésheng cāntīng, hǎo ma?
We'll go to the student canteen. What do you think?

Wǒmen qù xuésheng cāntīng ba!
Let's go to the student canteen!

15. qǐng "treat someone to"

In Chinese, if "qǐng" is used in some situations, such as inviting someone for a meal, a drink, or a movie, it implies that the person preceding "qǐng" will pay for someone else's food, drink, or entertainment. For example:

Tā qǐng wǒ chī fàn.	He'll treat me to a meal.
Wǒ qǐng nǐ hē kāfēi.	I'll treat you to coffee.
Nǐ qǐng wǒ kàn diànyǐng.	You'll treat me to a movie.

16. Nǐ tài huài le······

In general, a negative adjective used in the "tài······le" structure expresses disapproval. The example above, however, is not being used to make a negative judgment about a person's character; rather, it is being used to tease a person, as in the expression "You're bad" in English. The tone of "huài" should be softer in Chinese, as "Nǐ tài huài le~."

Exercises

I. Listen and write the price of the following items.

II. Make sentences by matching the words from Part I with those from Part II.

I	II
wǒ jiāo nǐ	qǐng nǐ chīfàn
xuésheng cāntīng de fàn	bīng nǎichá
wǒ xiǎng hē	hěn hǎo hē, yě hěn piányi
nàr de kāfēi	yòng kuàizi
jīntiān wǎnshang wǒ	tǐng hǎo chī de

III. Write the sentences with the words given.

1. chángcháng
2. hǎo chī
3. huì
4. yīnggāi
5. děi
6. ……de huà, (……) jiù……
7. suīrán……, dànshì……
8. suggestion, hǎo ma?

IV. Answer the following questions.

1. Nǐ chángcháng qù Xiānggǎng Dàxué lǐbian de cāntīng háishi wàibian de cāntīng chīfàn?
2. Nǐ xǐhuan Xiānggǎng Dàxué lǐbian de cāntīng ma?
3. Dàxué lǐbian de cāntīng guì bu guì?
4. Nǐ xǐhuan hē rè kāfēi háishi dòng nǎichá?
5. Nǐ xǐhuan chī shénme?
6. Nǐ huì yòng kuàizi chī fàn ma?
7. Nǐ xǐhuan yòng kuàizi chī fàn háishi yòng dāochā chī fàn?

V. Write a short passage.

If your family or your good friends come to Hong Kong to visit you, where will you take them to dinner and why? What food and drinks will you introduce them to? Please use the words we learned to write a short paragraph.

Culture Note

Table Manners in the Mainland and Hong Kong

A Chinese dining table is usually round so people can sit facing each other. The seats that face the door are reserved for the host and the most important guest. If you do not know where you should sit, you can wait to be shown. The seat at the left-hand side of the host is for the host's favored guest food, so the host can serve and pour wine for him or her. If you really do not eat what the host has served you, you need not reject it; you can let the host know your preference or just simply put it aside.

Chinese food is not served individually. Before the host orders, you may be asked what you would like to have. If you do not know how to use chopsticks, you can request a knife and fork. Bones and fish bones are to be placed on one's plate or on the table.

When pouring tea or wine, it should be done according to the sitting order. Always serve tea to other people before serving yourself. When people at the same table pour tea for you, you should say "Thank you!" What can you do if you are in the middle of a conversation when this happens? You can use your fingers to lightly tap on the table to express thanks.

Qi Bi, Shin-yee Cheung, and Gladys Leung, ed., *Food in Chinese Culture* (New York: Commercial Press [U.S.], 2009), 39. (slightly modified)

第四课　去哪儿吃饭?

学生1：你常常去哪儿吃饭?

学生2：我常常去星巴克旁边的学生餐厅吃饭。我们今天去那儿吃吧!

学生1：那个学生餐厅的东西好吃吗?

学生2：挺好吃的。那儿的茄蛋三文治很好吃。

学生1：用茄子做三文治?太奇怪了!太难吃了!

学生2：不是。那是番茄，不是茄子。

学生1：哦……

学生2：那儿的牛肉河粉和云吞面虽然不好吃，但是很便宜。

学生1：我不喜欢大学里边的餐厅。我常常去大学外边的餐厅。

学生2：哪个餐厅?贵不贵?

学生1：巴士站后边的餐厅很好。那儿的冰奶茶和热咖啡都很好喝，也很便宜。

学生2：太好了，我们今天晚上去那儿吃饭吧。我想喝冰奶茶。

学生1：在那儿吃饭的话，我们就得用筷子。你会用筷子吗?

学生2：哦……不太会。他们那儿有没有刀叉?

学生1：没有。你应该学习用筷子吃饭。

学生2：你教我，好吗?

学生1：你今天晚上请我吃饭的话，我就教你。

学生2：你太坏了……

5

My university life

Student 1 : I'm very busy and exhausted every day. How about you?

Student 2 : I think life as an exchange student is quite easy. Why are you so busy every day?

Student 1 : Because I have to spend a lot of time to learn Chinese and study Chinese culture, so I'm busy and tired.

Student 2 : Wow, you work so hard! What's your daily schedule like? When do you go to the Chinese language and culture classes every day?

měi tiān	每天	n.	everyday
lèi	累	adj.	tired; burned out
juéde	觉得	v.	to feel; to think
jiāohuàn shēng	交换生	n.	exchange student
shēnghuó	生活	n.	life
qīngsōng	轻松	adj.	easy; relaxing
wèi shénme	为什么	q.w.	why

Dì-wǔ kè

Dàxué shēnghuó

Xuésheng 1 : Wǒ měi tiān[1] dōu hěn máng, yě hěn lèi. Nǐ ne?

Xuésheng 2 : Wǒ juéde jiāohuàn shēng de shēnghuó tǐng qīngsōng de. Nǐ wèi shénme[2] měi tiān dōu hěn máng?

Xuésheng 1 : Wǒ yīnwei měi tiān dōu huā shíjiān xuéxí Hànyǔ hé Zhōngguó wénhuà, suǒyǐ hěn máng, yě hěn lèi.[3]

Xuésheng 2 : Nǐ tài nǔlì le! Nǐ de xuéxí shēnghuó zěnmeyàng? Měi tiān jǐ diǎn[4] shàng Hànyǔ kè hé Zhōngguó wénhuà kè?[5]

yīnwei	因为	conj.	because
suǒyǐ	所以	conj.	so; hence
huā	花	v.	to spend (time; money)
shíjiān	时间	n.	time
wénhuà	文化	n.	culture
nǔlì	努力	adj.	hardworking
jǐ diǎn	几点	q.w.	what time?
shàng kè	上课	v.	to go to class

Student 1 : I go to the Starbucks beside the library to speak Chinese with Chinese friends at 11:30 every morning and then see a Chinese movie with my girlfriend at 2:10 in the afternoon. At 7 p.m., I go to the Chinese canteen to have dinner with friends and then go to Lan Kwai Fong to have a drink with them. We drink and chat and then at 1:45 a.m. I go back to my dormitory to sleep.

shàngwǔ	上午	n.	morning
xiàwǔ	下午	n.	afternoon
diǎn	点	n.	o'clock; hour in time point
bàn	半	n.	half
túshūguǎn	图书馆	n.	library
gēn	跟	v.	with
shuō	说	v.	to speak; to say
fēn	分	n.	minute in time point
nǚ péngyou	女朋友	n.	girlfriend
kàn	看	v.	to see; to watch; to look
diànyǐng	电影	n.	movie

Xuésheng 1： Wǒ měi tiān shàngwǔ shíyī diǎn bàn[6] qù túshūguǎn pángbiān de Xīngbākè gēn[7] Zhōngguó péngyou shuō Hànyǔ. Xiàwǔ liǎng diǎn shí fēn gēn nǚ péngyou kàn Zhōngguó diànyǐng. Wǎnshang qī diǎn gēn péngyou qù Zhōng cāntīng chī fàn, ránhòu[8] qù Lánguìfāng hē jiǔ. Wǒmen yìbiān hē jiǔ yìbiān liáo tiānr.[9] Zǎoshang liǎng diǎn chà yíkè huí sùshè shuìjiào.

Zhōng cāntīng	中餐厅	n.	Chinese restaurant
ránhòu	然后	conj.	(first) . . . then
Lánguìfāng	兰桂坊	n.	Lan Kwai Fong
jiǔ	酒	n.	alcohol
yìbiān……yìbiān……	一边……一边……	conj.	while . . .
liáo tiānr	聊天儿	v.	to chat; to talk
zǎoshang	早上	n.	early morning
kè	刻	n.	a quarter (in a time point)
huí	回	v.	to return; to go back
shuìjiào	睡觉	v.	sleep

Student 2: That's your difficult school life?

Student 1: Yup. You have classes from Monday to Friday, but I have classes from Monday to Sunday. I'm very busy and exhausted, but I like my school life very much.

Student 2: I think all students would like your school life.

Xuésheng 2: Zhè shì nǐ de xuéxí shēnghuó?!

Xuésheng 1: Shì ya. Nǐmen cóng¹⁰ xīngqīyī dào¹⁰ xīngqīwǔ shàng kè, dànshì wǒ cóng xīngqīyī dào xīngqītiān dōu shàng kè. Suīrán fēicháng máng, yě fēicháng lèi, dànshì wǒ hěn xǐhuan¹¹ wǒ de xuéxí shēnghuó.

Xuésheng 2: Wǒ juéde měi ge xuésheng dōu xǐhuan nǐ de xuéxí shēnghuó.

cóng……dào……	从……到……		from . . . to . . .
xīngqīyī	星期一	n.	Monday
xīngqīwǔ	星期五	n.	Friday
xīngqītiān	星期天	n.	Sunday

Grammar

1. měi

"Měi" is a determinative meaning "each, every." It is always followed by a measure word such as "tiān" (day), meaning "every day." Other examples are as follows:

měi ge rén	each person
měi ge zhuānyè	each major

"Měi + m.w. (+ noun)" in Chinese indicates every case without exception, so "dōu" (see note 6, Chapter 2) can be a compound implying "in all cases." For example:

Wǒ měitiān dōu xuéxí Hànyǔ.
I study Chinese every day (without exception).

Měi ge rén dōu hē kāfēi.
Each person (without exception) drinks coffee.

Měi ge zhuānyè dōu hěn nán.
Every major (without exception) is difficult.

2. wèi shénme

"Wèi shénme" (why) is a question word (see note 7, Chapter 1) that is used to ask for an explanation. "Wèi shénme" always follows the subject, as in:

Nǐ wèi shénme měitiān dōu hěn máng?
Why are you very busy every day?

Tā wèi shénme bù xuéxí fǎlǜ?
Why doesn't he study law?

3. yīnwei……suǒyǐ……

The most common response to the "wèi shénme" question is the pattern "yīnwei (because)……suǒyǐ (therefore)." There are two constructions.

3.1 Subject + yīnwei + verb 1/adjective 1, suǒyǐ + verb 2/adjective 2.

Wǒ yīnwei měitiān dōu huā shíjiān xuéxí Hànyǔ, suǒyǐ hěn máng.
Because I spend time studying Chinese every day, (therefore) I am very busy.

Wǒ yīnwei hěn máng, suǒyǐ děi hē kāfēi.
Because I am very busy, (therefore) I have to drink coffee.

If the subject of the construction is the same, just like the examples above, the subject can be placed before or after "yīnwei."

3.2 When two different subjects occur in the construction, each subject will come after "yīnwei" and "suǒyǐ" respectively. For example:

yīnwei + subject 1 + verb 1, suǒyǐ + subject 2 + verb 2.
Yīnwei tā bù xiǎng chī sānwénzhì, suǒyǐ wǒmen bú qù xuésheng cāntīng.

Because he doesn't want to eat a sandwich, (therefore) we don't go to the student canteen.

4. jǐ diǎn

We discussed the question word "jǐ" in Chapter 2. "Jǐ" can be used to ask about a specific time point, date, or day of the week. As in:

4.1	Xiànzài jǐ diǎn?	What time is it?
	Xiànzài shí diǎn.	It's ten o'clock.
4.2	Jīntiān xīngqī jǐ?	What day is it today?
	Jīntiān xīngqī'èr.	Today is Tuesday.

Note that "liǎng" cannot be used in 4.2 because the pattern needs an ordinal number. "Xīngqī'èr" literally means "the second day of the week."

5. shàng kè

"Shàng" in "shàng kè" is a verb meaning "go to" and "kè" (class, lesson) is an object. This compound means "go to class" or "have a lesson." It can be split and a noun can be inserted between "shàng" and "kè." For example:

shàng Hànyǔ kè   take Chinese language lesson

6. Time points

In addition to the days, there are many particular time expressions in Chinese. The time point "hour" or "o'clock" is expressed by "diǎn" or "diǎn zhōng." The time point "minute" and "quarter of an hour" are "fēn" and "kè." The expression "half past" the time point "diǎn" (hour) is "bàn." The expression indicating "before" or "to" the time point "diǎn" (hour) uses "chà" (lit. "lack," "be short of" in Chinese), which can form a phrase before " diǎn." In summary:

	Time point	Part of Day	HH	MM	
6.1	6:15 a.m.	zǎoshang	liù diǎn		yíkè
6.2	12:30 p.m.	zhōngwǔ	shíèr diǎn		bàn
6.3	10:01 a.m.	shàngwǔ	shí diǎn	líng	yī
6.4	10:02 a.m.	shàngwǔ	shí diǎn	líng	èr
6.5	10:03 a.m.	shàngwǔ	shí diǎn	líng	sān
6.6	10:04 a.m.	shàngwǔ	shí diǎn	líng	sì
6.7	10:05 a.m.	shàngwǔ	shí diǎn	líng	wǔ
6.8	10:06 a.m.	shàngwǔ	shí diǎn	líng	liù
6.9	10:07 a.m.	shàngwǔ	shí diǎn	líng	qī
6.10	10:08 a.m.	shàngwǔ	shí diǎn	líng	bā
6.11	10:09 a.m.	shàngwǔ	shí diǎn	líng	jiǔ
6.12	10:10 a.m.	shàngwǔ	shí diǎn		shífēn
6.13	8:11 a.m.	shàngwǔ	bā diǎn		shíyī
6.14	2 p.m.	xiàwǔ	liǎng diǎn		Nil
6.15	6:40 p.m.	wǎnshang	liù diǎn		sìshí

Note:
- "Fēn" must be pronounced only when it comes after ten (see note 12 in the table).
- "Fēn" should NOT be placed after "bàn" or "kè" (see notes 1 and 2 in the table).
- "Líng" must be pronounced when the time point "minute" is between "HH:01" and "HH:09" (see from notes 3 to 11 in the table).
- When the time point "minute" is between "HH:40" and "HH:59," the "chà" construction is always used in Chinese. Taking "6:40" as an example (see note 15 in the table), it can also be expressed as "liù diǎn chà èrshí." "Fēn" is optional in this case. There are two ways to express the time point "HH:45." For example:
      8:45 jiǔ diǎn chà yíkè or bā diǎn sìshí wǔ.

7. gēn

"Gēn" literally means "follow." In general, "gēn + someone" preceding the main verb in Chinese is a propositional phrase. In this case, "gēn" and "hé" are similar. The construction is

    A + gēn + B + verbal phrase.

For example:

    Tā gēn péngyou hē kāfēi.
    He has coffee with his friend(s).

In the negative form, "bù" is placed before "gēn." As in:

    Tā bù gēn péngyou hē kāfēi.
    He doesn't have coffee with his friend(s).

8. Verb 1, ránhòu + verb 2

"Ránhòu" "and then" is used to connect two events or actions. It indicates an event that occurred or will occur after another event. For example:

    Wǒ qī diǎn gēn péngyou chīfàn, ránhòu qù Lánguìfāng.
    I will have a meal with my friend at seven o'clock, and then I will go to LKF.

9. yìbiān······yìbiān······

"Yìbiān + action 1 + yìbiān+action 2" is a sentence pattern indicating "do one thing while doing another thing."

    Wǒmen yìbiān hējiǔ yìbiān liáo tiānr.
    We drink wine while chatting.

    Tā yìbiān xuéxí Hànyǔ yìbiān chī sānwénzhì.
    He studies Chinese while eating a sandwich.

10. cóng······dào······

The pattern "cóng + time word 1 + dào + time word 2" can be used to mean "from time word 1 to time word 2." It gives force or emphasis to the scope of time, and "dōu" can be placed after the "cóng······dào······" pattern:

Wǒmen cóng xīngqīyī dào xīngqīwǔ dōu shàng kè.
We go to class from Monday to Friday.

Wǒ mèimei cóng shàngwǔ jiǔ diǎn dào xiàwǔ sān diǎn dōu hěn máng.
My younger sister is busy from 9 a.m. to 3 p.m.

11. xǐhuan

"Xǐhuan," meaning "like, enjoy," is a psychological verb that expresses a mental state.

If the answer is negative, you need to say

bù xǐhuan.

"Hěn" and other adverbs of degree that are used to express degree of modification can be placed in front of "xǐhuan." For example:

1. Wǒ tǐng xǐhuan kāfēi de.   I like coffee quite a lot.
2. Wǒ hěn xǐhuan kāfēi.   I like coffee very much.
3. Wǒ fēicháng xǐhuan kāfēi.   I really like coffee

Exercises

I. Decide whether the statements are true (T) or false (F).

1. Wáng Èrmíng hé Dīng Yīměi měi tiān dōu hěn máng. (   )
2. Wáng Èrmíng cóng xīngqīyī dào xīngqītiān dōu shàng Hànyǔ kè. (   )
3. Tāmen jīntiān wǎnshang yìqǐ qù Lánguìfāng hē jiǔ. (   )
4. Dīng Yīměi yě huì shuō pǔtōnghuà. (   )

II. Choose the correct answer.

1. Nǐ měitiān jǐ diǎn _____ Hànyǔ kè?
   A. zài   B. xué   C. shàng
2. Wǒ měi tiān _____ hěn máng.
   A. tài   B. tǐng   C. dōu
3. Wǒ měi tiān wǎnshang shíyī diǎn _____ shuìjiào.
   A. shí   B. kè   C. bàn
4. Jīntiān xiàwǔ wǒ _____ nǚ péngyou qù kàn diànyǐng.
   A. yòng   B. gēn   C. zài
5. _____ fēicháng máng, dànshì wǒ hěn xǐhuan wǒ de xuéxí shēnghuó.
   A. yīnwei   B. suǒyǐ   C. suīrán

III. Write the sentences with the words given.

1. ma   dōu   měi tiān   máng   nǐ   hěn
2. shuìjiào   wǒ   wǎnshang   sùshè   huí   shí diǎn   bàn
3. túshūguǎn   Xīngbākè   kāfēi   pángbiān   wǒ   zài   hē   de
4. yìbiān   yìbiān   wǒ   hē jiǔ   chī fàn
5. cóng   wǒ   xīngqīyī   xīngqītiān shàng   dào   kè   Hànyǔ   dōu

IV. Please answer the questions according to this timetable.

	xīngqīyī	xīngqī'èr	xīngqīsān	xīngqīsì	xīngqīwǔ	xīngqīliù hé xīngqītiān
8:30–9:20	chī fàn	chī fàn	chī fàn	chī fàn	chī fàn	chī fàn
9:30–12:20	Hànyǔ kè	Hànyǔ kè	Hànyǔ kè	Hànyǔ kè	Hànyǔ kè	mǎi dōngxi
14:30–17:20	diànyǐng kè	Zhōngguó wénhuà kè	diànyǐng kè	Zhōngguó wénhuà kè	diànyǐng kè	gēn péngyou kàn diànyǐng
18:00–19:30	shuō Hànyǔ	gēn péngyou chīfàn	shuō Hànyǔ	gēn péngyou chīfàn	shuō Hànyǔ	qù Zhōng cāntīng chī fàn
20:00–22:00	huí sùshè shuìjiào	huí sùshè shuìjiào	qù Lánguìfāng hē jiǔ	huí sùshè shuìjiào	huí sùshè shuìjiào	qù Lánguìfāng hē jiǔ

1. Wáng Èrmíng měi tiān zǎoshang jǐ diǎn chī zǎofàn?
2. Wáng Èrmíng xīngqī jǐ shàng Hànyǔ kè? (use "cóng……dào")
3. Wáng Èrmíng shénme shíhou* shàng diànyǐng kè?
4. Wáng Èrmíng xīngqīyī jǐ diǎn shàng Zhōngguó wénhuà kè?
5. Wáng Èrmíng shénme shíhou gēn péngyou chī fàn?
6. Wáng Èrmíng shénme shíhou gēn péngyou kàn diànyǐng?
7. Wáng Èrmíng shénme shíhou qù Lánguìfāng hē jiǔ?
8. Wáng Èrmíng shénme shíhou shuō Hànyǔ?

* shénme shíhou: when

Culture Note

The University of Hong Kong

The University of Hong Kong (HKU) is the territory's oldest institute of higher learning and an internationally recognised, research-led, comprehensive university. While recognising the strength of its heritage and traditions, HKU also engages in frontier research and academic endeavours that reflect and address the needs of a fast- changing, knowledge-based world.

The University of Hong Kong is the oldest tertiary education institution in Hong Kong. On March 16, 1910, Sir Frederick Lugard, the then Governor of Hong Kong, laid the foundation stone for the University. The University was first incorporated in Hong Kong as a self-governing body of scholars by the University Ordinance on March 30, 1911. On March 11, 1912, the University was officially opened, and Arts, Engineering and Medicine would become its first Faculties. The Faculty of Medicine evolved from the Hong Kong College of Medicine, founded in 1887. Of the College's early alumni, the most renowned was Dr Sun Yat-sen, often regarded as the founder of modern China. In December 1916, the University held its first congregation, with just 23 graduates.

Today, HKU has gained international recognition for its accomplishments as a research-led comprehensive university. From 2010 to 2012, the University held Centenary Celebrations to mark its 100th anniversary. In 2012—along with all the other institutions of higher learning in Hong Kong and in accordance with the government's education policy—the University officially launched its 4-year undergraduate curriculum. HKU continues to attract the best local students, along with many Mainland China and international students. The University's academics have outstanding achievements in teaching and research, and about half of HKU's faculty are from overseas. All ten faculties and their departments provide teaching and supervision for postgraduate-level research students, with administration undertaken by the Graduate School.

The University of Hong Kong website, accessed November 10, 2016, http://www.hku.hk/about/

第五课　大学生活

学生1：我每天都很忙，也很累。你呢？

学生2：我觉得交换生的生活挺轻松的。你为什么每天都很忙？

学生1：我因为每天都花时间学习汉语和中国文化，所以很忙，也很累。

学生2：你太努力了！你的学习生活怎么样？每天几点上汉语课和中国文化课？

学生1：我每天上午十一点半去图书馆旁边的星巴克跟中国朋友说汉语。下午两点十分跟女朋友看中国电影。晚上七点跟朋友去中餐厅吃饭，然后去兰桂坊喝酒。我们一边喝酒一边聊天儿。早上两点差一刻回宿舍睡觉。

学生2：这是你的学习生活？！

学生1：是呀。你们从星期一到星期五上课，但是我从星期一到星期天都上课。虽然非常忙，也非常累，但是我很喜欢我的学习生活。

学生2：我觉得每个学生都喜欢你的学习生活。

6
My roommate

My roommate came to Hong Kong in September of last year. His name is Zhang Xiaoming, and he is majoring in law. He comes from a family of three, his father, his mother, and him. Although he is from Beijing, he doesn't like eating Beijing roasted duck. He has gone to many places in China and eaten different kinds of food, but he mostly likes Sichuan food. He thinks Sichuan food is very hot, and it is extremely delicious. We often go to eat Sichuan hot pot together.

tóngwū	同屋	n.	roommate
qùnián	去年	n.	last year; previous year
jiǔyuè	九月	n.	September
dào	到	v.	to arrive (in/at)
Zhāng	张	n.	a Chinese surname
Běijīng	北京	n.	Beijing
Běijīng kǎoyā	北京烤鸭	n.	Beijing roasted duck
yìqǐ	一起	adv.	together
huǒguō	火锅	n.	hot pot
bùtóng	不同	adj.	different

Dì-liù kè

Wǒ de tóngwū

Wǒ tóngwū[1] shì qùnián jiǔyuè dào Xiānggǎng de.[2] Tā jiào Zhāng Xiǎomíng. Xiǎomíng xuéxí fǎlǜ zhuānyè. Tā jiā yǒu sān kǒu rén, bàba, māma hé tā. Tā suīrán shì Běijīng rén, dànshì bù xǐhuan chī Běijīng kǎoyā. Tā qùguo[3] hěnduō dìfang, yě chīguo hěnduō bùtóng fēngwèi de cài. Tā zuì xǐhuan chī Sìchuān cài. Tā juéde Sìchuān cài yòu má yòu là,[4] hǎo chī jí le.[5] Wǒmen chángcháng yìqǐ[6] qù chī Sìchuān huǒguō.

fēngwèi	风味	n.	flavor
Sìchuān	四川	n.	Sichuan Province
cài	菜	n.	dish/ cuisine
yòu……yòu……	又……又……	conj.	not only . . . but also . . .
má	麻	adj.	hot = causes a numbing sensation of the tongue and mouth
là	辣	adj.	spicy
jí le	极了		extremely

He is tall and handsome but not smart. Every day, Xiaoming is away from the dormitory because he either has lessons in the classroom or studies in the library. Even though he is very busy every day, he always helps me with my Chinese in the evening. Chinese is a little difficult (to learn). We speak Chinese every Monday, Wednesday, and Friday. We speak English every Tuesday, Thursday, and Saturday. On Sunday, I speak Chinese with him and he speaks English with me. Sometimes, he even teaches me how to write Chinese characters. We are not only roommates but also language partners.

Tā suīrán bù cōngming, dànshì yòu gāo yòu shuài. Tā měi tiān cóng shàngwǔ dào xiàwǔ dōu búzài sùshè. Tā bú shì zài jiàoshì li shàng kè, jiù shì[7] zài túshūguǎn li[8] xuéxí. Tā suīrán měi tiān dōu hěn máng, dànshì wǎnshang chángcháng bāngzhù wǒ xuéxí Hànyǔ.[9] Hànyǔ tǐng nán de. Wǒmen xīngqīyī, sān, wǔ[10] shuō Hànyǔ, èr, sì, liù shuō Yīngyǔ. Xīngqītiān, wǒ gēn[11] tā shuō Hànyǔ, tā gēn wǒ shuō Yīngyǔ. Yǒu shíhou,[12] tā jiāo wǒ xiě Hànzì. Wǒmen búdàn shì tóngwū, érqiě[13] yě shì xuéyǒu.

cōngming	聪明	adj.	clever; smart
gāo	高	adj.	tall
shuài	帅	adj.	handsome
bú shì……jiù shì	不是……就是	conj.	either . . . or . . .
jiàoshì	教室	n.	classroom
lǐ	里	n.	inside
bāngzhù	帮助	v.	to help; to assist
yǒu shíhou	有时候		sometimes
xiě	写	v.	to write
Hànzì	汉字	n.	Chinese character
xuéyǒu	学友	n.	learning partner
búdàn……érqiě	不但……而且	conj.	not only . . . but also

Grammar

1. "wǒ tóngwū" and "wǒ de tóngwū" (see note 5 in Chapter 1 and note 8 in Chapter 2)

Both "wǒ tóngwū" and "wǒ de tóngwū" are correct.

In previous lessons, we learned that "de" is a particle of modification and is always placed after personal pronouns, and "de" is dropped between a personal pronoun and words for relatives, friends, family (jiā), etc.

2. shì + t.w. + de

The structure "shì + t.w. + de" is used to emphasize the time of past events. "Shì" is placed before the part to be emphasized, and "de" is placed at the end of the sentence. The negative form is "bú shì······de."

For example:

> Wǒ tóngwū shì qùnián jiǔyuè dào Xiānggǎng de.
> My roommate came to Hong Kong in September last year.

> Tā shì wǎnshang shíyī diǎn shuìjiào de.
> He went to bed at 11 o'clock in the evening.

3. Verb + guo

The structure "verb + guo" is often used to emphasize that someone had such an experience in the past. The aspect particle "guo" with the neutral tone must come immediately after a verb.

For example:

> Wǒ qùguo Běijīng.
> I've been to Beijing.

> Wǒ chīguo Běijīng kǎoyā.
> I have eaten Beijing roasted duck.

> Wǒ xuéguo Hànyǔ.
> I have learned Chinese.

4. yòu······yòu······

The structure "yòu······yòu······," which means "not only . . . but also . . . ," indicates the actions, states, or features that exist at the same time. Verbs or adjectives can be used after yòu.

For example:

> Tā suīrán bù cōngming, dànshì yòu gāo yòu shuài.
> Although he's not intelligent, he is tall and handsome.

> Xīngbākè de kāfēi yòu hǎo hē yòu piányi.
> Starbucks coffee is not only tasty but also cheap.

> Tā zài cāntīng yòu chī yòu hē.
> He not only drinks but also eats in the canteen.

5. Adj. + jí le

"Jí le" means extremely. It should follow an adjective.

For example:

>Zhōngguó dà jí le.
>China is extremely big.

>Tā de Hànyǔ liúlì jí le.
>His Chinese is extremely fluent.

>Xiānggǎng piàoliang jí le.
>Hong Kong is extremely beautiful.

6. yìqǐ

"Yìqǐ" is an adverb. It means "with, together."

For example:

>Wǒmen yìqǐ xuéxí Hànyǔ.
>We learn Chinese together.

>Wǒmen yìqǐ shuō Yīngyǔ.
>We speak English together.

>Wǒmen yìqǐ chī wǔfàn.
>We eat lunch together.

7. bú shì……jiù shì……

"Bú shì……jiù shì……" means "either . . . or . . ." The expression is used before nouns, verbs, phrases, or clauses indicating that either statement is true. For example:

>Tā bú shì zài jiàoshì li shàngkè, jiù shì zài túshūguǎn li xuéxí.
>He either has lessons in the classroom or studies in the library.

>Tā bú shì Měiguó rén, jiù shì Yīngguó rén.
>She is either American or British.

>Wǒ bú shì hē bīng nǎichá, jiù shì hē rè kāfēi.
>I either drink the iced milk tea or the hot coffee.

8. "lǐ" localizer (see note 15, Chapter 2)

In a previous lesson, we learned the structure "subject + zài + place word + localizer."

For example, "Hànyǔ shū zài yǐzi xiàbian." Localizers that we have learned include "shàngbian" "on," "xiàbian" "under," "qiánbian" "front," "hòubian" "behind," "pángbiān" "beside," "lǐbian" "inside," and "wàibian" "outside." "Lǐ" is another localizer that means "in."

For example:

> Tā bú shì zài jiàoshì li shàngkè, jiù shì zài túshūguǎn li xuéxí.
> He either has lessons in the classroom or studies in the library.

> Wǒmen zài sùshè li liáo tiānr.
> We're chatting in the dormitory.

9. Pivotal sentence

A pivotal sentence has a predicate that is composed of two verbal phrases. The object of the first verb is also the subject of the second verb. For example, in the sentence "Tā jiāo wǒ xiě hànzì" (He teaches me how to write Chinese characters), "me" is the object of "teach," and it is the subject of "write."

For example:

> Wǎnshang wǒ qǐng nǐ chī fàn.
> I'll pay for your dinner.

> Wǒ jiāo nǐ yòng kuàizi.
> I'll teach you how to use chopsticks.

> Wǒ tóngwū chángcháng bāngzhù wǒ xuéxí Hànyǔ.
> My roommate always helps me with my Chinese.

Note that in the pivotal sentence, the first verb should be a verb with the meaning of "asking," "helping," or "teaching." In Chinese, they are "ràng," "bāngzhù," and "jiāo."

10. xīngqīyī, sān, wǔ

When we mention more than two days in a sentence, we normally use "xīngqī" only for first weekday. For the other weekdays that follow, "xīngqī" can be omitted. For example:

> Wǒmen xīngqīyī, sān, wǔ shuō Hànyǔ; èr, sì, liù shuō Yīngyǔ.
> We speak Chinese every Monday, Wednesday, and Friday. We speak English every Tuesday, Thursday, and Saturday.

11. gēn (see note 7, Chapter 5)

The preposition "gēn" is often used before a noun or a pronoun to make a prepositional phrase that means "together with," and it is always used before the predictive verb to indicate the manner of an action.

> gēn + pron./n. (person) + v. obj.

> Wǒ gēn tā shuō Hànyǔ, tā gēn wǒ shuō Yīngyǔ.
> I speak Chinese with him and he speaks English with me.

12. yǒu shíhou

"Yǒu shíhou," meaning "sometimes," can be placed either before or after the subject.

For example:

> Yǒu shíhou tā jiāo wǒ xiě Hànzì. Or Tā yǒu shíhou jiāo wǒ xiě Hànzì.
> Sometimes he teaches me how to write Chinese characters.

13. búdàn……érqiě……

The pattern "búdàn……érqiě……" is very similar to that of "not only … but also." It can be used to join two sentences together to highlight and reinforce the similarity between them.

For example:

> Tā búdàn huì shuō Yīngyǔ, érqiě yě huì shuō Hànyǔ.
> He can not only speak English but also Chinese.

> Búdàn tā huì shuō Hànyǔ, érqiě tā dìdi yě huì shuō Hànyǔ.
> Not only can he speak Chinese, but his younger brother can also speak Chinese.

> Tā búdàn shì wǒ de lǎoshī, érqiě háishi wǒ de péngyou.
> Not only is he my teacher, but he is also my friend.

Exercises

I. Listen to the dialogue and choose the correct answer.

1. Èrmíng de tóngwū shì nǎ guó rén?
   A. Zhōngguó rén   B. Yīngguó rén   C. Měiguó rén
2. Èrmíng xiànzài zài nǎr?
   A. túshūguǎn   B. jiàoshì   C. sùshè
3. Jīntiān xīngqī jǐ?
   A. xīngqīyī   B. xīngqīwǔ   C. xīngqīsì

II. Choose the correct words and fill in the blanks. Each word can be used only once.

suīrán……dànshì……   bù shì……jiù shì……   ……dehuà, jiù……
yīnwei……suǒyǐ……   yìbiān……yìbiān……   yòu……yòu……
Búdàn……érqiě……

1. Wǒ _____ zài Xīngbākè, _____ zài qù Xīngbākè de lùshang. (qù……de lùshang "on the way to …")
2. Nǐ chī _____ , wǒ _____ chī.
3. Wǒmen _____ hē jiǔ, _____ liáotiānr.
4. Wǒmen _____ shì tóngwū, _____ shì hǎo péngyou.
5. Nǐ de sùshè _____ hěn dà, _____ tài luàn le.
6. Wǒ nán péngyou _____ huì shuō Hànyǔ, _____ huì shuō Yīngyǔ.
7. Tā _____ měi tiān dōu huā shíjiān xuéxí Hànyǔ, _____ tā hěn máng.

III. Make sentences by matching the words from Part I with those from Part II.

I	II
Wǎnshang wǒ qǐng nǐ	shuìjiào
Tā jiāo wǒ	xuéxí Hànyǔ
Tā bāngzhù wǒ	xiě Hànzì
Tā huí sùshè	hē jiǔ
Wǒmen qù Lánguìfāng	chī fàn

IV. Rearrange the words to form coherent sentences.

1. sānyuè   dào   wǒ péngyou   de   shì   qùnián   Běijīng

   _____.

2. duō   qù   hěn   tā   guo

   _____.

3. suīrán   dànshì   xǐhuan   Běijīng rén   bù   wǒ   shì   Běijīng kǎoyā   chī

_____.

4. měi tiān   shàngwǔ   xiàwǔ   sùshè   Xiǎomíng   zài   cóng   dào   dōu

_____.

5. gēn   xīngqī   tā   yī   shuō   sān   wǒ   wǔ   Hànyǔ.

_____.

V. Read the passage and answer the questions.

Wǒ gēn wǒ de péngyou dōu shì jīnnián èryuè dào Xiānggǎng de. Tā jiào Dīng Yīměi, shì wǒ de péngyou, yě shì wǒ de tóngwū. Yīměi piàoliang jí le. Tā xuéxí jīngjì zhuānyè. Tā jiā yǒu sì kǒu rén, bàba, māma, gēge hé tā. Yīměi suīrán bú shì Zhōngguó rén, dànshì tā de Hànyǔ fēicháng hǎo. Wǒmen xīngqīyī, sān, wǔ wǎnshang qù túshūguǎn xuéxí, èr, sì, liù wǎnshang gēn péngyou qù Lánguìfāng hē jiǔ. Wǒmen suīrán měi tiān dōu hěn máng, dànshì wǒmen fēicháng xǐhuan Xiānggǎng de shēnghuó.

1. Tāmen shì jǐ yuè dào Xiānggǎng de?
2. Dīng Yīměi xuéxí shénme zhuānyè?
3. Dīng Yīměi piàoliang ma?
3. Dīng Yīměi de Hànyǔ hǎo ma?
4. Tāmen xīngqī jǐ qù túshūguǎn xuéxí? Xīngqī jǐ qù Lánguìfāng hē jiǔ?
5. Tāmen xǐhuan Xiānggǎng de shēnghuó ma?

VI. Write a short paragraph to introduce your roommate.

Culture Note

How to Find Housing and Rent Real Estate in Hong Kong

Real estate in Hong Kong is limited, and flats are notorious for being tiny and pricey. Most real-estate listings, whether to rent or buy, are done via a broker in Hong Kong.

Local realty agencies are camped out throughout the city and specialize in the areas they are located in. Actual offices will have the most up-to-date information, but websites give a good idea of what's on the market.

Hong Kong is divided into three main areas: Hong Kong Island, Kowloon Peninsula and New Territories—each with its own set of diverse neighborhoods. In general, Hong Kong Island is more affluent and home to some of the most expensive real estate in the city, especially in areas such as the Peak and Happy Valley. Popular expatriate neighborhoods include Mid-Levels (the area about halfway up Victoria Peak from the harbor, south of Central) and SoHo (which gets its name from being south of Hollywood Road in Central) on Hong Kong Island, because of its nightlife and proximity to Central.

Rental contracts in Hong Kong typically run two years. In the second year, though, either the tenant or landlord can often choose to terminate the lease penalty-free by giving two months' notice. Landlords are generally accustomed to negotiating clauses and terms in the lease, including rent price, furniture and appliances, and minor renovations. Your broker can often help with negotiations.

The broker's commission is usually equal to one month's rent, split 50-50 between the landlord and tenant. Most landlords require two months' worth of rent for a deposit and the first month's rent paid upfront.

Alice Truong, "How to Find Housing and Rent Real Estate in Hong Kong," *The Wall Street Journal*, December 28, 2010, accessed January 3, 2017, http://guides.wsj.com/hong-kong/guide-to-hong-kong/housing.

第六课　我的同屋

我同屋是去年九月到香港的。他叫张小明。小明学习法律专业。他家有三口人，爸爸、妈妈和他。他虽然是北京人，但是不喜欢吃北京烤鸭。他去过很多地方，也吃过很多不同风味的菜。他最喜欢吃四川菜。他觉得四川菜又麻又辣，好吃极了。我们常常一起去吃四川火锅。

他虽然不聪明，但是又高又帅。他每天从上午到下午都不在宿舍。他不是在教室里上课，就是在图书馆里学习。他虽然每天都很忙，但是晚上常常帮助我学习汉语。汉语挺难的。我们星期一、三、五说汉语，二、四、六说英语。星期天，我跟他说汉语，他跟我说英语。有时候，他教我写汉字。我们不但是同屋，而且也是学友。

7 The weather

Student 1 : What do you think of the weather in Hong Kong?

Student 2 : I think the winters are very comfortable but the summers are quite uncomfortable and often rainy. Do you like the winter in Hong Kong?

Student 1 : Actually, I think autumn is the most comfortable season in Hong Kong because it's not too hot or too cold. September and October are very cool and dry.

Student 2 : I like the summers here the least. It's hot and humid and very uncomfortable.

Student 1 : It's also a little uncomfortable in the spring here due to the humidity in April.

tiānqì	天气	n.	weather
dōngtiān	冬天	n.	winter
shūfu	舒服	adj.	comfortable
xiàtiān	夏天	n.	summer
zuì	最	adv.	the most
xià yǔ	下雨	v.	to rain
qiūtiān	秋天	n.	autumn
lěng	冷	adj.	cold

Dì-qī kè
Tiānqì

Xuésheng 1 : Nǐ juéde Xiānggǎng de tiānqì zěnmeyàng?

Xuésheng 2 : Wǒ juéde Xiānggǎng de dōngtiān hěn shūfu, xiàtiān zuì[1] bù shūfu, chángcháng xià yǔ. Nǐ xǐhuan Xiānggǎng de dōngtiān ma?

Xuésheng 1 : Wǒ juéde Xiānggǎng de qiūtiān bù lěng bú rè,[2] zuì shūfu. Jiǔyuè hé shíyuè yòu liángkuai yòu gānshuǎng.

Xuésheng 2 : Wǒ zuì bù xǐhuan zhèr de xiàtiān, yòu rè yòu cháoshī, hěn bù shūfu.

Xuésheng 1 : Zhèr de chūntiān yě yǒudiǎnr[3] bù shūfu. Sìyuè hěn cháoshī.

shíyuè	十月	n.	October
liángkuai	凉快	adj.	cool
gānshuǎng	干爽	adj.	cool and dry
cháoshī	潮湿	adj.	humid
chūntiān	春天	n.	spring
yǒudiǎnr	有点儿		a little (neg. adj.)
sìyuè	四月	n.	April

Student 2 : Because summer is not a comfortable season in Hong Kong, I'm going to take my summer vacation in mainland China.
Student 1 : You want to take your summer vacation in mainland China?! Don't you need to work? How rich you are!
Student 2 : Yes, I have to work as I'm only a poor student.
Student 1 : Which city are you going to work in?
Student 2 : Beijing. Even though the summer there is a little hot, it's not too humid.
Student 1 : I lived in Beijing for half a year. I like the autumn in Beijing very much because it's very cool.

dǎsuan	打算	v./n.	plan to do something; plan
nèidì	内地	n.	mainland China
guò	过	v.	spend (a vacation)
shǔjià	暑假	n.	summer vacation
búyòng	不用	v.	not need to do

Xuésheng 2 : Yīnwei Xiānggǎng de xiàtiān hěn bù shūfu, suǒyǐ wǒ dǎsuan[4] jīnnián qù nèidì guò shǔjià.

Xuésheng 1 : Nǐ xiǎng qù nèidì guò[5] shǔjià?! Búyòng gōngzuò ma? Nǐ zhēn yǒu qián[6]······

Xuésheng 2 : Bú shì. Wǒ shì yí ge qióng xuésheng, suǒyǐ, wǒ děi gōngzuò.

Xuésheng 1 : Nǐ dǎsuan zài nǎ ge chéngshì gōngzuò?

Xuésheng 2 : Běijīng. Nàr de xiàtiān suīrán yǒudiǎnr rè, kěshì bú tài cháoshī.

Xuésheng 1 : Wǒ zài Běijīng zhùguo bàn nián.[7] Wǒ hěn xǐhuan Běijīng de qiūtiān, hěn liángkuai.

zhēn	真	adv.	really, truly, very
yǒu qián	有钱	adj.	rich
qióng	穷	adj.	poor
chéngshì	城市	n.	city; urban area
kěshì	可是		but

Student 2 : How's the winter in Beijing? Does it snow?

Student 1 : The winter in Beijing is really cold. It often snows. It's a very interesting city and I like it very much.

Student 2 : I like it too, but my parents don't like Beijing very much. They're very worried about me.

Student 1 : Why are they worried about you?

Student 2 : My father heard that the air quality in Beijing isn't good. My mother heard that the water in Beijing isn't clean. They worry that I may get sick and have stomach problems.

Student 1 : Don't worry. I didn't get stomach problems and was fine when I was in Beijing. I didn't get sick, and you'll be fine, too.

sǐ le	死了		extremely
xià xuě	下雪		snowy
dānxīn	担心	v.	to worry (about); to be anxious
tīngshuō	听说	v.	(someone) heard
kōngqì	空气	n.	air
shuǐ	水	n.	water

Xuésheng 2 : Běijīng de dōngtiān zěnmeyàng? Xià xuě ma?

Xuésheng 1 : Běijīng de dōngtiān lěng sǐ le,⁸ chángcháng xià xuě.⁹ Zhè ge chéngshì hěn yǒu yìsi, wǒ hěn xǐhuan.

Xuésheng 2 : Wǒ yě hěn xǐhuan, kěshì wǒ bàba māma bú tài xǐhuan Běijīng. Tāmen hěn dānxīn¹⁰ wǒ.

Xuésheng 1 : Tāmen wèi shénme dānxīn nǐ?

Xuésheng 2 : Wǒ bàba tīngshuō¹¹ Běijīng de kōngqì bù hǎo. Wǒ māma tīngshuō Běijīng de shuǐ bù gānjing. Tāmen hěn dānxīn wǒ zài nàr shēng bìng,¹² lā dùzi.

Xuésheng 1 : Búyòng¹³ dānxīn……wǒ zài Běijīng de shíhou¹⁴ méiyou lā dùzi,¹⁵ yě méiyou juéde bù shūfu. Wǒ méiyou shēng bìng, nǐ yě bú huì¹⁶ shēng bìng.

gānjing	干净	adj.	clean
shēng bìng	生病	v.	to be sick; to have a sickness
lā dùzi	拉肚子	v.	diarrhea
zài……de shíhou	在……的时候		when
méiyou	没有	v.	to have not experienced the situation before
huì	会		will; shall; be going to …

Grammar

1. zuì

"Zuì" means "the most." It is often used as an adverbial before an adjective or an optative verb to show the superlative degree in a group of people or things. Note that adjectives do not have a distinct superlative form. To express the superlative meaning, precede the adjectival verb with the intensifier "zuì."

For example:

Xiānggǎng de dōngtiān hěn shūfu, xiàtiān zuì bù shūfu.

The winter is very comfortable, but summer is the most uncomfortable season in Hong Kong.

Wǒ zuì bù xǐhuan zhèr de xiàtiān.

I like summers here the least.

2. bù adj. + bù adj.

bù lěng bú rè/bú dà bù xiǎo

The construction "bù + adj. (1) + bù + adj. (2)" means "neither . . . nor," just the right size or degree.

For example:

Nà bēi chá bù lěng bú rè.

That cup of tea is neither too cold nor too hot.

Nà tiáo qúnzi bú dà bù xiǎo, hěn héshì.

That dress is neither too big nor too small. It's just right.

Nà ge cāntīng bú jìn bù yuǎn.

That restaurant is neither too close nor too far.

3. yǒudiǎnr + adj. (negative)

"Yǒu (yì) diǎnr" meaning "somewhat, a little bit," is often used before certain adjectives or verbs indicating moderation, and often implies dissatisfaction or negation.

For example:

Zhèr de chūntiān yǒudiǎnr bù shūfu.

It's a little uncomfortable in spring here.

Nàr de xiàtiān suīrán yǒudiǎnr rè, kěshì bú tài cháoshī.

Even though the summer there is a little hot, it's not too humid.

Xīngbākè de kāfēi yǒudiǎnr guì.

The coffee at Starbucks is a little expensive.

4. dǎsuan

"Dǎsuan" means "plan, to plan, to intend to." It can be used as a noun or a verb.

For example:

"Dǎsuan" as a verb:
> Wǒ dǎsuan jīnnián qù nèidì guò shǔjià.
> I'm planning to have my summer vacation in mainland China.

"Dǎsuan" as a noun:
> Nǐ jīnnián shǔjià yǒu shénme dǎsuan?
> What are your plans for this summer vacation?

5. guò

"Guò" means "to spend (time), to celebrate (a birthday, a festival)."

For example:

> Wǒ dǎsuan jīnnián qù nèidì guò shǔjià.
> I'm going to have my summer vacation in mainland China.

> Wǒ dǎsuan zài Xiānggǎng guò nián.
> I plan to spend New Year in Hong Kong.

6. Nǐ zhēn yǒu qián! "You're really rich!"

"Zhēn" here means really.

For example:

> Nǐ zhēn cōngming.
> You are really smart.

> Tā de Hànyǔ zhēn hǎo.
> His Chinese is really good.

> Wǒ māma zhēn máng.
> My mother is really busy.

7. Verb + guo + time duration

The construction "verb + guo + time duration" is used to indicate the duration of an action or a state that has already taken place. The expression refers to the action that has been experienced.

For example:

> Wǒ zài Běijīng zhùguo sān nián.
> I lived in Beijing for three years.

> Wǒ xuéguo Fǎyǔ.
> I learned French (before).

> Wǒ chīguo Zhōngguó cài.
> I've eaten Chinese food (before).

8. adj. + sǐ le (complement of degree)

The construction "adj. + sǐ le" is used to express a high degree, and "sǐ le" here is similar to extremely.

For example:

> Wǒ máng sǐ le.
> I am extremely busy.
>
> Tā è sǐ le.
> She is extremely hungry.
>
> Wǒ kě sǐ le.
> I am extremely thirsty.

Note that a neutral or negative adjective is always used in the pattern.

9. xià yǔ/xià xuě

"Xià yǔ" and "xià xuě" are a "verb + object" structure. You can put an adjective or "num. + m.w." between the verb and the object.

For example:

> Xià dà yǔ.
> It's raining heavily.
>
> Xià dà xuě.
> It snows heavily.

10. dānxīn

"Dānxīn" means "to worry about, anxious." It can be used as a verb or an adjective.

For example:

> "Dānxīn" as an verb:
>
> > Wǒ bàba māma hěn dānxīn wǒ.
> > My parents are very worried about me.
> >
> > Tāmen wèi shénme dānxīn nǐ?
> > Why are they worried about you?
>
> "Dānxīn" as a verb:
>
> > Tāmen hěn dānxīn Běijīng de kōngqì bùhǎo.
> > They worry that the air quality in Beijing is not good.
> >
> > Tāmen hěn dānxīn wǒ zài nàr shēng bìng, lā dùzi.
> > They worry that I may get sick like getting diarrhea there.

11. tīngshuō

"Tīngshuō" means "heard."

For example:

> Wǒ bàba tīngshuō Běijīng de kōngqì bùhǎo.
> My father heard that the air quality in Beijing isn't good.

> Wǒ māma tīngshuō Běijīng de shuǐ bù gānjing.
> My mother heard that the water in Beijing isn't clean.

> Wǒ tīngshuō nǐ shì Běijīng rén.
> I heard that you're from Beijing.

12. shēng bìng

"Shēng bìng" means "be sick," "have an illness."

For example:

> Wǒ shēng bìng le.
> I am sick.

> Wǒ méiyou shēng bìng.
> I am not sick.

13. búyòng (see note 8, Chapter 3)

In the previous chapter, we learned that one of the functions of "yòng" in Chinese is "use," and that "búyòng" "not use" is the negative form. For example:

> Wǒ búyòng shǒujī.
> I don't use a cell phone.

Here, "búyòng" has another meaning: "don't need to do something."

For example:

> Wǒ jīntiān búyòng gōngzuò.
> I don't need to work today.

Another example is "búyòng xiè." It literally means "don't need to thank." This phrase is used as a response to an expression of thanks, meaning "you're welcome."

14. zài……de shíhou

In Chinese, when we talk about events that happened at or during a particular time, "de shíhou" is usually used, meaning "when" or "while." The structure is:

> (Sub.) + v./adj. + de shíhou, subj. + v. + obj.

Note that, as a time expression, a clause with "de shíhou" should be placed at the beginning of the sentence. The time word can appear either before or after the subject.

For example:

> Wǒ zài Běijīng de shíhou méiyou lā dùzi.
> I didn't get diarrhea when I was in Beijing.

> Xuéxí lèi de shíhou, wǒ xǐhuan hē kāfēi.
> I like to have a cup of coffee when I'm tired of studying.

> Wǒ chī fàn de shíhou xǐhuan kàn diànyǐng.
> I like to watch movies while I'm eating (or having a meal).

15. méiyou + v. (see note 9, Chapter 2)

In the previous chapter, we learned that "méiyou" means "have not," when it is followed by a noun. For example, "Wǒ méiyou gēge."

When "méiyou" is followed by a verb, it indicates that an action has not taken place. Do not use "bù" as the marker of negation, and do not use "le" after a verb when talking about an action that did not happen.

For example:

> Wǒ méiyou shēng bìng.
> I didn't get sick.

> Wǒ méiyou hē píjiǔ.
> I didn't drink beer.

> Wǒ zài Běijīng de shíhou méiyou lā dùzi, yě méiyou juéde bù shūfu.
> I didn't get diarrhea and I was fine when I was in Beijing.

16. huì (see note 12, Chapter 4)

In the previous chapter, we learned "huì," which means "know how to." For example, "Wǒ huì yòng kuàizi."

Here, "huì," an auxiliary verb that indicates possibility, is usually placed before a verb. "Bú huì," "not possible, impossible," is the negative form. For example:

> Wǒ méiyou shēng bìng, nǐ yě bú huì shēng bìng.
> I didn't get sick and you will be fine, too.

> Jīntiān wǎnshang wǒ huì qù kàn diànyǐng.
> I am going to watch a movie tonight.

Exercises

I. Listen to the dialogue and choose the correct answer.

1. Běijīng de nǎ ge jìjié (season) zuì shūfu?
   A. chūntiān   B. xiàtiān   C. qiūtiān
2. Xiǎomíng xǐhuan Xiānggǎng de dōngtiān ma?
   A. xǐhuan   B. bù xǐhuan
3. Shànghǎi de tiānqì zěnmeyàng?
   A. xiàtiān hěn lěng   B. dōngtiān hěn rè   C. chūntiān hé qiūtiān hěn shūfu

II. Choose the correct words and fill in the blanks. Each word can be used only once.

dǎsuan	guo	děi	búyòng	dānxīn
shēng bìng	lā	sǐ le	zhēn	tīngshuō

1. Wǒ _____ Xiānggǎng de chūntiān hěn cháoshī.
2. Wǒ zài Běijīng de shíhou méiyou _____, yě méiyou _____ dùzi.
3. Wǒmen _____ míngtiān qù chī Běijīng kǎoyā.
4. Wǒ méiyou qián, shì yí ge qióng xuésheng, suǒyǐ wǒ _____ gōngzuò.
5. Tā hěn yǒu qián, suǒyǐ _____ gōngzuò.
6. Nǐ _____ yǒu qián!
7. Wǒ bàba māma hěn _____ wǒ.
8. Xiānggǎng de xiàtiān rè _____.
9. Jīnnián xiàtiān, Xiǎomíng huì qù nèidì _____ shǔjià.

III. Make sentences with the words given.

1. juéde……zěnmeyàng
2. yǒu diǎnr
3. dǎsuan
4. tīngshuō
5. zài……de shíhou
6. suīrán……kěshì……

IV. This is the weather report of Hong Kong, Beijing, Shanghai, and Harbin on December 24, 2015. Please decide whether the statements are true (T) or false (F).

2015 Nián 12 Yuè 24 Rì			
Hong Kong	Beijing	Shanghai	Harbin
↓ 21°C ↑ 25°C	↓ –6°C ↑ 6°C	↓ 10°C ↑ 18°C	↓ –30°C ↑ –15°C
22°C	0°C	16°C	–20°C
99%	30%	50%	10%

1. Xiānggǎng de dōngtiān zuì rè, zuì cháoshī. (   )
2. Běijīng de dōngtiān zuì lěng, zuì gānshuǎng. (   )
3. Shànghǎi de dōngtiān bú rè yě bù lěng, hěn shūfu. (   )
4. Hā'ěrbīn(Harbin) de dōngtiān hěn rè, bù shūfu. (   )

V. Answer the following questions.

1. Nǐ juéde Xiānggǎng de tiānqì zěnmeyàng?
2. Nǐ juéde Xiānggǎng de kōngqì zěnmeyàng?
3. Nǐ zuì xǐhuan Xiānggǎng de nǎ ge jìjié (season)? Wèi shénme?
4. Nǐ dǎsuan qù nǎr guò shǔjià?
5. Shǔjià de shíhou, nǐ dǎsuan gōngzuò ma?
6. Nǐ zuì xǐhuan nǎ ge chéngshì? Wèi shénme?

VI. Write a short paragraph to introduce the weather in your country. Use the following words.

chūntiān	xiàtiān	qiūtiān	dōngtiān	rè	lěng	liángkuai	cháoshī
gānshuǎng	shūfu	bù shūfu	xǐhuan	xià	yǔ	xià	xuě

Culture Note

The 24 Seasonal Division Points

The names for the 24 seasonal division points are: Beginning of Spring, Rain Water, Waking of Insects, Vernal Equinox, Pure Brightness, Grain Rain, Beginning of Summer, Grain Budding, Grain in Ear, Summer Solstice, Slight Heat, Great Heat, Beginning of Autumn, Limit of Heat, White Dew, Autumnal Equinox, Cold Dew, Frost's Descent, Beginning of Winter, Slight Snow, Great Snow, Winter Solstice, Slight Cold, and Great Cold, respectively.

The Beginning of Spring, Beginning of Summer, Beginning of Autumn and Beginning of Winter mark the start of the four seasons. The Vernal Equinox and the Autumnal Equinox are the two points at which day and night are equal.

Summer Solstice is the longest day and shortest night in a year; the opposite is true for Winter Solstice.

Rain Water means the start of the spring rains. The Waking of Insects indicates that the spring thunder awakens hibernating insects.

Pure Brightness means the onset of spring when a bright and clean spring scene replaces the cold, withered, and yellow scene in winter.

Grain Rain indicates that, from that day, there will be more rainfall, which is beneficial to the growth of crops.

Grain Budding shows that crops that will ripen in summer start to show plump seeds.

Grain in Ear tells people that the wheat has ripened.

Slight Heat and Great Heat indicate the full onset of summer, Great Heat being the hottest day of the season.

Limit of Heat shows that scorching summer days will soon be gone.

White Dew tells people that dew appears in the morning to show that the weather is turning cold, and as this intensifies, we move on to Cold Dew.

Frost's Descent means the appearance of the first frost of the season.

Slight Snow and Great Snow mean the arrival of the snowy season.

Slight Cold and Great Cold indicate the degree of cold in winter, Great Cold being the coldest day of the season.

Ren Qiliang, ed., *Chinese Common Knowledge Series—Culture* (Hong Kong: Hong Kong China Tourism Press, 2005), 54–55.

第七课　天气

学生1：你觉得香港的天气怎么样?

学生2：我觉得香港的冬天很舒服，夏天最不舒服，常常下雨。你喜欢香港的冬天吗?

学生1：我觉得香港的秋天不冷不热，最舒服。九月和十月又凉快又干爽。

学生2：我最不喜欢这儿的夏天，又热又潮湿，很不舒服。

学生1：这儿的春天也有点儿不舒服。四月很潮湿。

学生2：因为香港的夏天很不舒服，所以我打算今年去内地过暑假。

学生1：你想去内地过暑假?！不用工作吗? 你真有钱!

学生2：不是。我是一个穷学生，所以，我得工作。

学生1：你打算在哪个城市工作?

学生2：北京。那儿的夏天虽然有点儿热，可是不太潮湿。

学生1：我在北京住过半年。我很喜欢北京的秋天，很凉快。

学生2：北京的冬天怎么样? 下雪吗?

学生1：北京的冬天冷死了，常常下雪。这个城市很有意思，我很喜欢。

学生2：我也很喜欢，可是我爸爸妈妈不太喜欢北京。他们很担心我。

学生1：他们为什么担心你?

学生2：我爸爸听说北京的空气不好。我妈妈听说北京的水不干净。他们很担心我在那儿生病，拉肚子。

学生1：不用担心。我在北京的时候没有拉肚子，也没有觉得不舒服。我没有生病，你也不会生病。

8
Yin cha

Student 1 : Where do you often eat?

Student 2 : Starbucks. I like the salad and sandwiches there.

Student 1 : Starbucks' food is good, but we can't eat it that often. I like yin cha better.

Student 2 : Yin cha? You mean to drink tea? I can't just drink tea without eating

Student 1 : The term "yin cha" in Guangzhou doesn't mean only drinking tea but drinking tea while eating dianxin.

Student 2 : Dianxin? I liked dianxin the most when I was in Beijing.

Dì-bā kè
Yǐn chá

Xuésheng 1 : Nǐ chángcháng qù nǎr chī fàn?

Xuésheng 2 : Xīngbākè. Wǒ xǐhuan nàr de shālǜ hé sānwénzhì.

Xuésheng 1 : Xīngbākè de dōngxi suīrán hěn hǎo, kěshì bù néng[1] cháng chī. Wǒ juéde yǐn chá tǐng jiànkāng de.

Xuésheng 2 : Yǐn chá?[2] Hē chá? Wǒ bù néng zhǐ[3] hē chá, bù chī fàn.

Xuésheng 1 : Guǎngdōng de yǐn chá bú shì zhǐ hē chá, ér shì[4] yìbiān hē chá yìbiān chī diǎnxin.

Xuésheng 2 : Diǎnxin? Wǒ zài Běijīng de shíhou, zuì xǐhuan chī diǎnxin.

shālǜ	沙律	n.	salad
néng	能		can do something (physically)
yǐn chá	饮茶	v.	to drink tea and eat dim sum in Guangzhou or Hong Kong; yumcha
jiànkāng	健康	adj.	healthy
zhǐ	只	adv.	only; just
Guǎngdōng	广东	n.	Guangdong Province
bú shì……ér shì……	不是……而是……	conj.	not this, but . . .
diǎnxin	点心	n.	dim sum

Student 1 : Cantonese dim sum is different from northern dianxin. Some Cantonese dim sum is sweet and some is salty. All northern dianxin is sweet.

Student 2 : Which do you think is tastier? Cantonese dim sum or northern dianxin?

Student 1 : I think Cantonese dim sum is tastier than northern dianxin. I like shrimp dumplings, barbecued pork buns, and fengzhao the most.

Student 2 : Fengzhao? What's fengzhao?

Student 1 : Fengzhao are chicken feet.

Student 2 : What?! You eat chicken feet? That sounds horrible!

gēn……(bù) yíyàng	跟……不一样	conj.	A is (not) the same as B.
běifāng	北方	n.	northern part
yǒu de……yǒu de……	有的……有的……		some of them . . . some of them . . .
tián	甜	adj.	sweet
xián	咸	adj.	salty
bǐ	比	prep./v.	compared to / to compare to

Xuésheng 1 : Guǎngdōng diǎnxin gēn běifāng de diǎnxin bù yíyàng.⁵ Yǒu de Guǎngdōng diǎnxin shì tián de, yǒu de Guǎngdōng diǎnxin shì xián de.⁶ Běifāng de diǎnxin dōu shì tián de.

Xuésheng 2 : Nǐ juéde Guǎngdōng diǎnxin hǎo chī háishi⁷ běifāng de diǎnxin hǎo chī?

Xuésheng 1 : Wǒ juéde Guǎngdōng diǎnxin bǐ⁸ běifāng de hǎo chī. Wǒ zuì xǐhuan xiājiǎo, chāshāo bāo hé fèngzhǎo.

Xuésheng 2 : Fèngzhǎo? Fèngzhǎo shì shénme?

Xuésheng 1 : Fèngzhǎo jiùshì⁹ jī jiǎo.

Xuésheng 2 : Shénme?! Nǐ chī jī de jiǎo?! Tài kěpà le······

xiājiǎo	虾饺	n.	shrimp dumplings
chāshāo bāo	叉烧包	n.	barbecued pork bun
fèngzhǎo	凤爪	n.	(lit.) phoenix feet
jī	鸡	n.	chicken
jiǎo	脚	n.	foot; feet (plural)
kěpà	可怕	adj.	horrible

Student 1 : No, they're not horrible. Fengzhao are not only tender but also tasty and healthy. You should try it.

Student 2 : Excuse me, I have to go to the washroom. There's something wrong with my stomach . . .

Student 1 : Are you kidding? No worries. I'll take you to the best-known restaurant in Hong Kong for yin cha and you can try it.

Student 2 : Well, okay. But, I don't want to try fengzhao. I'll take a picture of it.

Xuésheng 1 : Bù kěpà. Fèngzhǎo búdàn yòu ruǎn yòu hǎo chī, érqiě duì shēntǐ hěn hǎo,[10] nǐ zuìhǎo[11] shìshi.

Xuésheng 2 : Duìbuqǐ, wǒ děi qù xǐshǒujiān. Wǒ de wèi hěn bù shūfu……

Xuésheng 1 : Zhēn de ma?[12] Búyòng dānxīn, míngtiān wǒ dài nǐ qù[13] Xiānggǎng zuì yǒu míng de cāntīng yǐn chá. Nǐ kěyǐ chángchang.

Xuésheng 2 : En, hǎo ba. Búguò,[14] wǒ bù xiǎng cháng fèngzhǎo. Wǒ yào gěi fèngzhǎo pāi yì zhāng zhàopiàn.

ruǎn	软	adj.	soft; tender
zuìhǎo	最好		best
shìshi	试试	v.	to try
duìbuqǐ	对不起		excuse me; sorry
xǐshǒujiān	洗手间	n.	washroom
wèi	胃	n.	stomach
yǒu míng	有名	adj.	famous
chángchang	尝尝	v.	to taste
búguò	不过	conj.	however
gěi	给	v.	to give
pāi	拍	v.	to take (photo)

Grammar

1. néng

"Néng," as an optative verb, means "to be able to do something physically." It is often used before verbs to express the ability or possibility. The negative form is usually "bù néng." For example:

> Nǐ néng hē jiǔ ma?
> Can you drink alcohol?

> Wǒ néng hē jiǔ.
> I can drink alcohol.

> Kuàicān suīrán hěn hǎo chī, dànshì wǒmen bù néng cháng chī.
> Fast food is tasty, but we can't eat it that often.

2. yǐn chá

"Yǐn" means "to drink," and "chá" means "tea," so "yǐn chá" literally means "drink tea." Nowadays, we say "hē chá" for "drink tea." "Yǐn chá" means "going for dim sum," which includes drinking Chinese tea and having dim sum. It is very popular in Guangdong Province and in Hong Kong.

3. zhǐ

"Zhǐ," meaning "only or just," is used before a verb.

For example:

> Wǒ bùnéng zhǐ hē chá, bù chī fàn.
> I can't just drink tea without eating something.

> Wǒ zhǐ xǐhuan chī sānwénzhì.
> I just like eating sandwiches.

> Wǒ zhǐyǒu yí ge jiějie.
> I just have one elder sister.

4. bú shì······ér shì

The structure "bú shì······ér shì," meaning "it is not . . . but," is used to connect or contrast two words, phrases, or clauses. It emphasizes the affirmed part rather than negated part.

For example:

> Guǎngdōng de yǐn chá bú shì zhǐ hē chá, ér shì yìbiān hē chá yìbiān chī diǎnxin.
> Yincha in Cantonese culture does not just mean "drinking tea" but rather "drinking tea" while "eating dim sum."

> Wǒ xiànzài bú shì xuésheng le, ér shì lǎoshī.
> I'm not a student anymore but a teacher now.

5. gēn……yíyàng

The structure "gēn……yíyàng" indicates that two noun phrases are the same or similar in a particular property. If they are different, the structure "gēn……bù yíyàng" is used.

Noun 1+ gēn + Noun 2 + (bù) yíyàng

Subject	gēn	N/Pr	(bù)yíyàng
Wǒ bàba	gēn	wǒ māma	yíyàng.
Wǒ de sùshè	gēn	nǐ de (sùshè)	yíyàng.
Xīngbākè de kāfēi	gēn	xuéxiào cāntīng de (kāfēi)	bù yíyàng.
Guǎngdōng de diǎnxin	gēn	běifāng de (diǎnxin)	bù yíyàng.

Note that if the two nouns indicating the two items being compared are the same, the second noun can be omitted.

6. yǒu de……yǒu de……

"Yǒu de," as a modifier, often means "some (of) . . ." and can be used independently. It can also be used two or three times in consecutive clauses within a sentence. For example:

Yǒu de Guǎngdōng diǎnxin shì tián de, yǒu de (Guǎngdōng diǎnxin) shì xián de.

Note that the second "Guǎngdōng diǎnxin" can be omitted, since the noun has been used in the previous sentence.

Zài Xiānggǎng Dàxué, yǒude xuésheng shì Rìběn rén, yǒude (xuésheng) shì Yīngguó rén, yǒude (xuésheng) shì Měiguó rén.

In the University of Hong Kong, some students are from Japan, some students are from the United Kingdom, and some students are from the United States.

7. háishi (see note 8, Chapter 3)

"Háishi" is used only when asking someone to choose between alternatives. For example:

	Question		Answer
Alternative A	háishi	Alternative B	
Nǐ juéde Guǎngdōng de diǎnxin hǎo chī	háishi	běifāng de diǎnxin hǎo chī?	Wǒ juéde běifāng de diǎnxin hǎo chī. (Alternative B)
Nǐ dǎsuan zuò dìtiě	háishi	(zuò) bāshì?	Wǒ dǎsuan zuò bāshì. (Alternative B)
Tā xuéxí fǎlǜ	háishi	(xuéxí) jīngjì?	Tā xuéxí jīngjì. (Alternative B)

Note that if the verb has been used in the first clause, it can be omitted in the second clause.

8. bǐ

The preposition "bǐ" is used to compare the qualities and characteristics of two things. It means "compared with something, it is . . ." "Bǐ" and its object are often placed before an adjective in a sentence. If the two nouns indicating the two items being compared are the same, the second noun can be omitted.

Subj. + bǐ + n./pron. + adjective

Subject	bǐ	N./Pron.	Adjective
Kāfēi	bǐ	nǎichá	guì.
Nǐ de sùshè	bǐ	wǒ de (sùshè)	dà.
Guǎngdōng diǎnxin	bǐ	běifāng de (diǎnxin)	hǎo chī.

9. jiù shì

"Jiù" can be used to emphasize or confirm a fact or stress that "this is indeed the fact." For example:

Fèngzhǎo jiù shì jī jiǎo.
Fengzhao are (surely) chicken feet.

Tā jiù shì wǒ mèimei.
She is (surely) my younger sister.

Zhè jiù shì Dīng lǎoshī.
This is (surely) teacher Ding.

10. duì……hěn hǎo

The construction "duì……hěn hǎo" means "it is good for something or someone."

For example:

Chī fèngzhǎo duì pífū hěn hǎo.
Eating chicken feet is good for your skin.

Yùndòng duì shēntǐ hěn hǎo.
Working out is good for your health.

Hē shuǐ duì shēntǐ hěn hǎo.
Drinking water is good for health.

11. zuìhǎo + v.

The construction "zuìhǎo + v." means "the best way is . . ."

For example:

Nǐ zuìhǎo shìshi fèngzhǎo.
You should try chicken feet.

Nǐ shǔjià zuìhǎo qù Běijīng xuéxí Hànyǔ.
In summer vacation, you should go to Beijing to study Chinese.

Nǐ zuìhǎo xiànzài zhǎo gōngzuò.
You should find a job now.

12. zhēn de ma?

"Zhēn de ma?" means "really?"

For example:

> Zhēn de ma? Míngtiān wǒmen qù Shāndǐng?
> Really? We'll go to the Peak tomorrow?
>
> Wǒmen qù chī fèngzhǎo, zhēn de ma?
> We'll go to eat chicken feet? Really?
>
> Tā shì Měiguó rén, kěshì huì shuō Hànyǔ, zhēn de ma?
> He's American, but he can speak Chinese. Really?

13. dài (somebody) qù (someplace)

The construction "dài somebody qù someplace" means "bring or take someone to someplace."

For example:

> Wǒ dài nǐ qù cāntīng.
> I'll take you to the restaurant.
>
> Tā dài wǒ qù jiàoshì.
> He brings me to the classroom.
>
> Lǎoshī dài wǒmen qù dìtiě zhàn.
> The teacher brings us to the MTR station.

14. búguò

"Búguò" means "but, yet, however, only."

For example:

> Wǒ xiǎng chī diǎnxin, búguò wǒ bú yào fèngzhǎo.
> I want to eat dim sum, but I don't want to eat chicken feet.
>
> Wǒ xiǎng hē diǎnr dōngxi, búguò wǒ bù xiǎng hē chá.
> I want to drink something, but I don't want to drink tea.
>
> Wǒ xiǎng qù lǚxíng, búguò wǒ bù xiǎng zuò fēijī.
> I want to travel, but I don't want to take the airplane.

Exercises

I. Listen to the dialogue and choose the correct answer.

1. Xiǎomíng zhè ge xīngqītiān dǎsuan zuò shénme?
   A. qù kàn diànyǐng   B. qù túshūguǎn   C. qù chī Xiānggǎng diǎnxin

2. Xiǎomíng zhè ge xīngqītiān dǎsuan qù nǎr)
   A. Zhōnghuán (Central)   B. Jiānshāzuǐ (Tsim Sha Tsui)   C. Wàngjiǎo (Mongkok)

3. Xiǎomíng zuì xǐhuan chī shénme?
   A. xiājiǎo   B. chāshāo bāo   C. fèngzhǎo

4. Yīměi zhè ge xīngqītiān dǎsuan zuò shénme?
   A. qù kàn diànyǐng   B. qù yǐn cha   C. qù chī Běijīng kǎoyā

II. Choose the correct words and fill in the blanks. Each word can be used only once.

| néng | zhǐ | bǐ | gēn | jiù shì |
| yǒude | háishi | tèbié | yíxia | |

1. Wǒ de sùshè _____ nǐ de sùshè dà.
2. Nǐ bù _____ zhǐ hē jiǔ, bù chī fàn.
3. Guǎngdōng de diǎnxin _____ Běijīng de diǎnxin bù yíyàng.
4. Nǐ kěyǐ shì _____.
5. Nǐ xǐhuan hē kāfēi _____ Zhōngguó chá?
6. Fèngzhǎo de wèidào hěn _____.
7. _____ xuésheng shì Běijīng rén, yǒude shì Xiānggǎng rén.
8. Tā _____ wǒ mèimei.
9. Wǒ _____ huì shuō Yīngyǔ, bú huì shuō Hànyǔ.

III. Make sentences with the words given.

1. bú shì……ér shì……
2. gēn……bù yíyàng
3. háishi
4. juéde
5. ……bǐ……
6. jiù shì

IV. Make sentences according to the pictures.

1. Kāfēi bǐ nǎichá _____.
2. Nǎichá bǐ kāfēi _____.

1. Chāshāo bāo bǐ xiājiǎo _____.
2. Xiājiǎo bǐ chāshāo bāo _____.

Hong Kong	Beijing
↓21°C ↑25°C	↓-6°C ↑6°C
22°C	0°C
99%	30%

1. Xiānggǎng de dōngtiān bǐ Běijīng de dōngtiān _____.
2. Běijīng de dōngtiān bǐ Xiānggǎng de dōngtiān _____.

1. Xiānggǎng Dàxué de sùshè bǐ Běijīng Dàxué de _____.
2. Běijīng Dàxué de sùshè bǐ Xiānggǎng Dàxué de_____.

1. Xīngbākè de kāfēi bǐ xuéxiào cāntīng de kāfēi _____.
2. Xīngbākè de kāfēi shíjiǔ kuài qián, bǐ xuéxiào cāntīng de kāfēi _____.

V. Answer the following questions.

1. Nǐ chángcháng qù nǎr chī fàn?
2. Nǐ wèi shénme xǐhuan / bù xǐhuan qù Xiānggǎng Dàxué de cāntīng chī fàn?
3. Nǐ xǐhuan chī Guǎngdōng de diǎnxin ma?
4. Nǐ juéde Guǎngdōng de diǎnxin guì ma?
5. Nǐ chángcháng chī Zhōngcān (Chinese food) háishi Xīcān (Western food)?

VI. Write a short paragraph to introduce the yin cha culture in Hong Kong. Use the following words.

xǐhuan	yǐn chá	hē chá	chī fàn	diǎnxin	chāshāo bāo
fèngzhǎo	tián	xián	hǎo chī	piányi	xiājiǎo

Culture Note

Shrimp Dumplings (Har Gow) and Minced Pork with Shrimp Dumplings (Siu Mai)

"Drinking tea" for breakfast is one of Cantonese people's special customs. For Cantonese people, "drinking tea" means being at a teahouse in the morning and having tea delicacies called dim sum.

Dim sum has many different varieties. Shrimp dumplings, called *har gow*, and minced pork with shrimp dumplings, called *siu mai*, are two of the most famous dim sum dishes. In areas outside Guangdong, there are dishes that are very similar too. The appearance of *har gow* is similar to that of *jiaozi* from other areas. In northern China, there's a dish called *shaomai* that looks similar to *siu mai*. However, *har gow* and *siu mai* have features that distinguish them as Cantonese cuisine.

First of all, they are made to look exquisite and small in size, much smaller than *jiaozi* and *shaomai*. Eating a few will not make you feel too full. Furthermore, *har gow* wrappings are transparent, making them very beautiful to look at.

In addition, there are shrimp in the fillings of both *har gow* and *siu mai*. Because Guangdong has a lot of rivers and is located close to the sea, Cantonese people like to eat food from the rivers and the sea.

Qi Bi, Shin-yee Cheung, and Gladys Leung, ed., *Food in Chinese Culture* (New York: Commercial Press [U.S.], 2009), 23.

第八课　饮茶

学生1：你常常去哪儿吃饭？

学生2：星巴克。我喜欢那儿的沙律和三文治。

学生1：星巴克的东西虽然很好，可是不能常吃。我觉得饮茶挺健康的。

学生2：饮茶？喝茶？我不能只喝茶，不吃饭。

学生1：广东的饮茶不是只喝茶，而是一边喝茶一边吃点心。

学生2：点心？我在北京的时候，最喜欢吃点心。

学生1：广东点心跟北方的点心不一样。有的广东点心是甜的，有的广东点心是咸的。北方的点心都是甜的。

学生2：你觉得广东点心好吃还是北方的点心好吃？

学生1：我觉得广东点心比北方的好吃。我最喜欢虾饺、叉烧包和凤爪。

学生2：凤爪？凤爪是什么？

学生1：凤爪就是鸡脚。

学生2：什么？！你吃鸡的脚？！太可怕了……

学生1：不可怕。凤爪不但又软又好吃，而且对身体很好，你最好试试。

学生2：对不起，我得去洗手间。我的胃很不舒服……

学生1：真的吗？不用担心，明天我带你去香港最有名的餐厅饮茶。你可以尝尝。

学生2：嗯，好吧。不过，我不想尝凤爪。我要给凤爪拍一张照片。

9
Reading week

Student 1 : Next week is reading week. What are you going to do?
Student 2 : My parents and my girlfriend will take a trip to Hong Kong together.
Student 1 : You should go to Causeway Bay first and walk around the shopping mall, and then go to Ocean Park to see the animals.
Student 2 : Unfortunately, they're hard to deal with. My parents don't like to walk around shopping malls, and my girlfriend doesn't like animals.
Student 1 : I see. If you go to the shopping mall, your parents won't be happy. If you go to Ocean Park, your girlfriend won't be happy.

xià ge xīngqī	下个星期	n.	next week
yuèdú zhōu	阅读周	n.	reading week
fùmǔ	父母	n.	parents; father and mother
lái	来	v.	to come
lǚyóu	旅游	v.	to travel

Dì-jiǔ kè

Yuèdú zhōu

Xuésheng 1 : Xià ge xīngqī[1] shì yuèdú zhōu. Nǐ dǎsuan zuò shénme?

Xuésheng 2 : Wǒ fùmǔ hé nǚ péngyou yìqǐ[2] lái[3] Xiānggǎng lǚyóu.

Xuésheng 1 : Nǐmen yīnggāi xiān qù Tóngluówān guàng[4] shāngchǎng, zài qù Hǎiyáng Gōngyuán kàn dòngwù.

Xuésheng 2 : Tāmen dōu hěn máfan.[5] Wǒ fùmǔ bù xǐhuan guàng shāngchǎng. Wǒ de nǚ péngyou bù xǐhuan dòngwù.

Xuésheng 1 : Míngbai le. Qù shāngchǎng dehuà, nǐ fùmǔ jiù bù gāoxìng. Qù Hǎiyáng Gōngyuán dehuà, nǚ péngyou jiù bù gāoxìng.

xiān……zài……	先……再……	conj.	first . . . and then . . .
Tóngluówān	铜锣湾	n.	Causeway Bay
guàng	逛	v.	to stroll; to visit
shāngchǎng	商场	n.	shopping mall
Hǎiyáng Gōngyuán	海洋公园	n.	Ocean Park
dòngwù	动物	n.	animal
máfan	麻烦	adj.	annoyed

Student 2 : Yes. If they're all unhappy, I'm unhappy. Do you have any good ideas?

Student 1 : Let me think about it. On the first day, take them to Lama Island and have fun. On the second day, go to see the Buddha on Lantau Island. On the third day, go to the Peak and see the ocean view of Victoria Harbour. It's very beautiful, especially the night view. And on the fourth day, have seafood in Sai Kung.

zhǔyi	主意	n.	idea
dì	第	n.	number
dì-yī tiān	第一天		the first day
dài	带	v.	take someone to someplace
Nányādǎo	南丫岛	n.	Lama Island
wánr	玩儿	v.	to play
Dàyǔshān	大屿山	n.	Lantau Island

Xuésheng 2 : Shì de. Tāmen dōu bù gāoxìng dehuà, wǒ jiù bù gāoxìng. Nǐ yǒu shénme hǎo zhǔyi?

Xuésheng 1 : Wǒ xiǎngxiang[6]······dì-yī[7] tiān, nǐ dài tāmen qù Nányādǎo wánr, dì-èr tiān qù Dàyǔshān kàn dà fó, dì-sān tiān qù Shāndǐng kàn Wéigǎng* de hǎijǐng, tèbié shì[8] yèjǐng, fēicháng piàoliang, dì-sì tiān qù Xīgòng chī hǎixiān.

* Wéigǎng = The full Chinese name is "Wéi duō lì yà gǎng."

dà fó	大佛	n.	Buddha
Shāndǐng	山顶	n.	the Peak
Wéigǎng	维港	n.	Victoria Harbour
hǎijǐng	海景	n.	sea view
yèjǐng	夜景	n.	night view
tèbié	特别	adj./adv.	special/especially
Xīgòng	西贡	n.	Sai Kung
hǎixiān	海鲜	n.	seafood

Student 2 : That's a good suggestion. We'll be tired but very happy. What are you going to do during reading week?

Student 1 : I spent my reading week alone in Hong Kong last semester. It was boring. So this reading week, my friends and I are going to take a trip to Thailand.

Student 2 : Wow! I went to Thailand last year. Here are some pictures I took. Thailand is an interesting place and Thai food is amazing. I really like it.

Student 1 : I wish I could go to Thailand right now!

Xuésheng 2 : Zhè ge zhǔyi tǐng hǎo de. Wǒmen suīrán hěn lèi, kěshì dōu hěn gāoxìng. Nǐ yuèdú zhōu dǎsuan zuò shénme?

Xuésheng 1 : Shàng ge xuéqī wǒ shì yí ge rén[9] zài Xiānggǎng guò yuèdú zhōu de, yǒudiǎnr wúliáo, suǒyǐ zhè ge yuèdú zhōu wǒ hé péngyou dǎsuan yìqǐ qù Tàiguó lǚyóu.

Xuésheng 2 : À! Qùnián shǔjià wǒ qùle[10] Tàiguó. Zhè shì zhàopiàn. Tàiguó hěn yǒu yìsi, nàr de cài hěn tèbié,[11] wǒ hěn xǐhuan.

Xuésheng 1 : Wǒ zhēn xiǎng mǎshàng[12] qù Tàiguó!

xuéqī	学期	n.	semester
yí ge rén	一个人		alone; by oneself
wúliáo	无聊	adj.	boring
Tàiguó	泰国	n.	Thailand

Grammar

1. xià ge xīngqī

"Xià" means "next." For example:

xià ge xīngqī	next week
xià ge xīngqīyī	next Monday
xià ge yuè	next month

"Gè" is the measure word for "xīngqī" "week" and "yuè" "month." For example:

one week	yí ge xīngqī
two months	liǎng ge yuè
next day	míngtiān
next week	xià (ge) xīngqī
next Monday	xià (ge) xīngqīyī
next month	xià ge yuè
next year	míngnián

Note that the measure word "gè" can be omitted in the phrase "xià ge xīngqī" but cannot be omitted in the phrase" xià ge yuè." For "next day" or "next year," we say "míngtiān," "míngnián" instead of "xià tiān," "xià nián." Do not place "gè" in front of "tiān" or "nián."

2. yìqǐ

"Yìqǐ," meaning "together," is always used before a verb. For example:

Wǒ fùmǔ hé nǚ péngyou yìqǐ lái Xiānggǎng lǚyóu.

My parents and my girlfriend will travel to Hong Kong together.

Wǒ hé wǒ péngyou yìqǐ kàn diànyǐng.

My friend and I watch the movies together.

3. lái

"Lái" means "to come."

"Lái + place word" means "come to a place."

For example:

Wǒ fùmǔ hé nǚ péngyou yìqǐ lái Xiānggǎng lǚyóu.

My parents and my girlfriend will come to Hong Kong together and take a trip.

Note that there are two or more verbs or verb phrases that refer to the same subject in the above sentence. This is known as a serial-verb construction in Chinese. In this textbook, the construction commonly represents two consecutive actions.

4. guàng

"Guàng" means "to stroll, to visit." For example:

Nǐmen yīnggāi xiān qù Tóngluówān guàng shāngchǎng.
You should go shopping in Causeway Bay first.

5. máfan

"Máfan" means "troublesome, annoying." It can be used as an adjective. For example:

Tāmen hěn máfan.
They're very annoying.

6. xiǎngxiang (see note 5, Chapter 3)

In the previous chapters, we learned that "xiǎng," which means "would like," can be used before another verb as a modal verb. For example:

Wǒ xiǎng mǎi yì píng píjiǔ.
I'd like to buy a bottle of beer.

"Xiǎngxiang" means "think (about)"; "wǒ xiǎngxiang" means "let me think (about it)."

For example:

Wǒ xiǎngxiang jīntiān wǎncān chī shénme.
Let me think about what we are going to eat for dinner.

7. dì-yī

To make a number ordinal, add the prefix "dì" before the number. For example:

dì-yī	first
dì-yī tiān	the first day
dì-sān kè	the third lesson

8. tèbié shì

"Tèbié shì" means especially.

For example:

Tèbié shì yèjǐng,……
Especially the night view, . . .

Xiānggǎng de diǎnxin hěn hǎo chī, tèbié shì xiājiǎo.
Dim sum in Hong Kong is very delicious, especially the shrimp dumplings.

Tāmen de Yīngyǔ dōu hěn liúlì, tèbié shì Zhāng Xiǎomíng.
Their English are very fluent, especially Zhang Xiaoming's.

9. yí ge rén

"Yí ge rén" means "alone, by oneself." For example:

Wǒ dǎsuan yí ge rén zài Xiānggǎng guò yuèdú zhōu.

I'm going to spend reading week in Hong Kong by myself.

10. le

In this lesson, the particle "le" can be used after a verb to indicate completion of an event or action. It can be used for the event or action that happens in the past, present, or future. If a specific object is placed after the "verb-le" pattern, there is no need to add another clause to the sentence. For example:

Subject + Verb + le + Specific Place

Qùnián shǔjià wǒ qùle Tàiguó.

Last year I went to Thailand.

Subject + Verb +le + Number + Measure Word + Noun

Wǒ mǎile sān ge píngguǒ.

I bought three apples.

Subject + Verb + le + Adjective + Noun

Wǒ zuótiān huāle hěnduō qián.

I spent a lot of money yesterday.

If the object does not refer to any specific item, another clause should be placed after the verb-le clause. As in:

subj. + $v._1$ + le + $obj._1$ + $v._2$ + $obj._2$

One of the functions of "le" is to express that, after completing the first action, the second action will start. For example:

Míngtiān wǒ chīle fàn qù dàxué.

Tomorrow after lunch/dinner, I'll go to the university.

In spoken Chinese, the object(s) can be omitted.

11. tèbié

"Tèbié" is used as an adjective which means special.

For example:

Tā hěn tèbié.

She's very special.

Xiānggǎng hěn tèbié.

Hong Kong is very special.

12. mǎshàng "immediately"

"Mǎshàng," meaning immediately, as soon as possible, is an adverb that precedes a verb. For example:

Wǒ zhēn xiǎng mǎshàng qù Tàiguó!
I wish I could go to Thailand immediately!

Nǐ mǎshàng qù cāntīng.
You need to go to the canteen immediately.

Exercises

I. Listen to the dialog and decide whether the statements are true (T) or false (F).

1. Xiǎomíng hé tā de bàba māma bú qù Shāndǐng. (   )
2. Xiǎomíng dǎsuan dài tā de bàba māma qù chī diǎnxin. (   )
3. Yīměi dǎsuan qù Běijīng lǚyóu. (   )
4. Běijīng chūntiān de tiānqì bù shūfu. (   )
5. Yīměi dǎsuan shì yíxià Běijīng kǎoyā. (   )

II. Choose the correct words and fill in the blanks. Each word can be used only once.

shàng ge   xià ge   yìqǐ   jiù   zài   tèbié   dài   le   máfan

1. Qù nián shǔjià wǒ qù _____ Běijīng.
2. Xiānggǎng de hǎixiān hěn guì, _____ shì Xīgòng de hǎixiān.
3. Wǒ dǎsuan xiān qù Běijīng, _____ qù Shànghǎi (Shanghai).
4. _____ yuèdú zhōu wǒ shì yí ge rén zài Xiānggǎng guò de.
5. Nǚ péngyou bù gāoxìng dehuà, wǒ _____ bù gāoxìng.
6. Wǒ nǚ péngyou hěn _____.
7. _____ xīngqī shì yuèdú zhōu, nǐ dǎsuan zuò shénme?
8. Wǒ dǎsuan _____ wǒ fùmǔ qù Dàyǔshān kàn dà fó.
9. Jīntiān wǎnshang wǒmen _____ qù chī fàn hǎo ma?

III. Write the sentences with the words given.

1. ……dehuà, jiù……
2. dài someone qù someplace
3. xiān……, zài……
4. máfan
5. zhǔyi

IV. Choose the correct answer.

Xià ge xīngqī _1_ yuèdú zhōu, wǒ dǎsuan hé péngyou yìqǐ _2_ Běijīng lǚyóu. Tīngshuō Běijīng _3_ piàoliang, _4_ hěn yǒu yìsi, Běijīng de tiānqì yě hěn _5_ . Wǒmen dǎsuan _6_ fēijī (airplane) qù Běijīng. Wǒmen dǎsuan dì-yī tiān qù _7_ Běijīng kǎoyā, dì-èr tiān qù _8_ jīngjù (Beijing opera), dì-sān tiān qù _9_ shāngchǎng, dì-sì tiān qù Gùgōng (the Forbidden City). Wǒ zhēn xiǎng _10_ qù Běijīng.

1. A. bù   B. shì   C. hěn
2. A. qù   B. zài   C. guò
3. A. hěn   B. shì   C. búshì
4. A. bù   B. yě   C. shì
5. A. shūfu   B. piàoliang   C. yǒu yìsi
6. A. kàn   B. zuò   C. hé
7. A. hē   B. kàn   C. chī
8. A. kàn   B. guàng   C. wánr
9. A. kàn   B. guàng   C. wánr
10. A. mǎshàng   B. fēicháng   C. hěn

V. Write a short passage.

Suppose your friend will come to Hong Kong to visit you. Please use the words we have learned to describe where you will take him or her, what you are going to do, and why.

Culture Note

The Territory of China

China has a land area of about 9.6 million km² and is the third largest country in the world, next to Russia and Canada. The nation also has 3 million km² of territorial waters. At present, China has 23 provinces, 5 autonomous regions, 4 municipalities, and 2 special administrative regions directly under the central government. The capital city is Beijing.

From north to south, the territory of China spans over 50 degrees of latitude, stretching from the center of the Heilongjiang River north of the town of Mohe in Heilongjiang Province to Zengmu Reef at the southernmost tip of the Nansha Islands. China extends 5,500 km from north to south. When northeast China is in deep winter, Hainan Island in the south is still enjoying summer. China has a broad territory, abundant resources, and beautiful mountains and rivers.

第九课　　阅读周

学生1：下个星期是阅读周。你打算做什么？

学生2：我父母和女朋友一起来香港旅游。

学生1：你们应该先去铜锣湾逛商场，再去海洋公园看动物。

学生2：他们都很麻烦。我父母不喜欢逛商场。我的女朋友不喜欢动物。

学生1：明白了。去商场的话，你父母就不高兴。去海洋公园的话，女朋友就不高兴。

学生2：是的。他们都不高兴的话，我就不高兴。你有什么好主意？

学生1：我想想……第一天，你带他们去南丫岛玩儿，第二天去大屿山看大佛，第三天去山顶看维港*的海景，特别是夜景，非常漂亮，第四天去西贡吃海鲜。

学生2：这个主意挺好的。我们虽然很累，可是都很高兴。你阅读周打算做什么？

学生1：上个学期，我是一个人在香港过阅读周的，有点儿无聊，所以这个阅读周我和朋友打算一起去泰国旅游。

学生2：啊！去年暑假我去了泰国。这是照片。泰国很有意思，那儿的菜很特别，我很喜欢。

学生1：我真想马上去泰国！

* 维港 = The full Chinese name is "维多利亚港".

10
May I ask how to get to the library?

Student 1 : May I ask how to get to the library?

Student 2 : (*Pointing at the campus map.*) This is the campus map. We're in front of the bank. So, walk straight ahead and turn left when you reach the supermarket, and then continue walking straight. Then turn right at Starbucks. The library is just behind Starbucks.

xiàoyuán	校园	n.	campus
dìtú	地图	n.	map
xiànzài	现在	n.	now; currently
yínháng	银行	n.	bank
yìzhí	一直	adv.	keep straight
zǒu	走	v.	to walk

Dì-shí kè

Qǐngwèn, zěnme qù túshūguǎn?

Xuésheng 1 : Qǐngwèn, zěnme qù túshūguǎn?

Xuésheng 2 : (*Zhǐ zhe xiàoyuán dìtú*) Zhè shì xiàoyuán dìtú. Wǒmen xiànzài zài yínháng de qiánbian. Nǐ yìzhí[1] zǒu, dàole[2] chāoshì wǎng[3] zuǒ guǎi,[4] ránhòu,[5] yìzhí zǒu, dàole Xīngbākè wǎng yòu guǎi. Túshūguǎn jiù[6] zài Xīngbākè hòubian.

chāoshì	超市	n.	supermarket
wǎng	往	v.	toward
zuǒ	左	n.	left
zuǒ guǎi	左拐		turn left
yòu	右	n.	right
jiù	就	adv.	exactly
máfan	麻烦	adj.	annoyed

Student 1 : I see. Also, how can I get to Central?

Student 2 : You need to go to Central by bus, so keep walking straight and turn right when you reach the supermarket. Then go out of the university gate and cross the street. The bus stop is just on the opposite side of the university gate. You can take either a bus or a mini bus to get to Central. You can also take a taxi or the MTR. The taxi stop is just next to the bus stop.

Xuésheng 1 : Ò. Wǒ zěnme qù Zhōnghuán ne?
Xuésheng 2 : Nǐ děi zuò[7] bāshì qù Zhōnghuán. Nǐ yìzhí zǒu, dàole chāoshì wǎng yòu guǎi. Chū[8] xiàomén, guò[9] mǎlù, bāshì zhàn jiù zài dàxué xiàomén duìmiàn.[10] Dàbā, xiǎobā dōu dào Zhōnghuán. Nǐ yě kěyǐ zuò dīshì huòzhě dìtiě, dīshì zhàn jiù zài bāshì zhàn pángbiān.

Zhōnghuán	中环	n.	Central
chū	出	v.	to go out of
xiào	校	n.	school; university
mén	门	n.	gate; door
guò	过	v.	to cross
mǎlù	马路	n.	street; road
duìmiàn	对面	n.	the opposite side
dàbā	大巴	n.	bus
xiǎobā	小巴	n.	mini bus

Student 1 : Got it. Thank you.

Student 2 : You're welcome. Where are you going now?

Student 1 : I'll go to the library first.

Student 2 : I'm going there too. Let me take you there.

Student 1 : Great! Thank you very much!

Student 2 : You're welcome. Let's go!

[In the taxi.]

Driver   : Hello. Where would you like to go?

Student : Hello. I want to go to Central Station. Thanks.

Driver   : Sure, no problem.

[Ten minutes later.]

Driver   : Here we are. Thirty-five dollars.

Student : Ok. Here it is.

Driver   : You gave me fifty dollars, so that's fifteen dollars' change. Your Chinese is good!

Student : Oh, it's nothing. (I'm flattered.)

Xuésheng 1 : Míngbai le. Xièxie.

Xuésheng 2 : Bú kèqi. Nǐ xiànzài dǎsuan qù nǎr?

Xuésheng 1 : Wǒ xiān qù túshūguǎn.

Xuésheng 2 : Wǒ yě qù túshūguǎn. Wǒ dài nǐ qù ba.

Xuésheng 1 : Tài hǎo le! Tài máfan[11] nǐ le!

Xuésheng 2 : Bú kèqi. Wǒmen zǒu ba.

[Zài dīshì shang]

Sījī   : Nínhǎo, qǐngwèn nín qù nǎr?

Xuésheng : Nínhǎo, wǒ yào qù Zhōnghuán dìtiě zhàn, xièxie.

Sījī   : Hǎo de; méi wèntí.

[Shí fēnzhōng hòu]

Sījī   : Nín dào le. Yígòng sānshíwǔ kuài.

Xuésheng : Hǎo de, gěi nín qián.[12]

Sījī   : Nín gěi wǒ wǔshí kuài; wǒ zhǎo nín shíwǔ kuài.[13] Nín de Hànyǔ zhēn hǎo!

Xuésheng : Nǎli nǎli.[14]

tài máfan nǐ le	太麻烦你了		(I) bother you too much. This is another way to show gratitude.
wèntí	问题	n.	problem; question
zhǎo	找	v.	to give change
nǎli nǎli	哪里哪里		Not at all. (A response to thanks or praise in a polite way.)

Grammar

1. yìzhí

The adverb "yìzhí" can be used to indicate space, which means going continuously in one direction. For example:

    yìzhí zǒu   go straight

    Nǐ yìzhí zǒu, dào chāoshì wǎng zuǒ guǎi, ránhòu yìzhí zǒu.

"Yìzhí" can also be used to indicate time, which means an action, continues without any interruption or a state without any change within a period of time. For example:

    Tā zuótiān yìzhí hěn máng.

    He was busy for the whole day yesterday.

    Tā zuìjìn yìzhí hěn máng.

    He has been busy recently.

2. dào

The verb "dào" means "to arrive"; it can be used before nouns. For example:

    Nǐ yìzhí zǒu, dào chāoshì wǎng zuǒ guǎi.

    Walk straight ahead and turn left when you arrive at the supermarket.

    Dào Xīngbākè wǎng yòu guǎi.

    Turn right when you arrive at Starbucks.

    Wǒmen dào jiā le.

    We've arrived home.

3. wǎng "toward"

The preposition "wǎng" together with a noun that indicates place or direction is used to indicate the direction of the action.

    wǎng yòu guǎi "turn right"

    wǎng zuǒ guǎi "turn left"

4. dàole chāoshì wǎng zuǒ guǎi

This is the grammar we learned in Chapter 9. The particle "le" can be used after a verb to indicate completion of an event or action. The second clause or phrase always indicates that a new event or action will start.

For example:

> Nǐ dàole chāoshì wǎng zuǒ guǎi.
> When you get to the supermarket, turn left.
>
> Nǐ xiàle kè lái zhǎo wǒ.
> After you've finished class, come see me.
>
> Wǒmen chīle wǎnfàn qù kàn diànyǐng.
> After we've finished dinner, we'll go to see a movie.

5. xiān……ránhòu

"Xiān v.p.$_1$……ránhòu v.p.$_2$", "first v.p.$_1$, and then v.p.$_2$" is the pattern indicating the sequence of events. For example:

> Wǒmen xiān xué dì-shí kè de shēngcí, ránhòu xuéxí yǔfǎ.
> We'll learn the new words in lesson 10 first and then learn the grammar.
>
> Wǒ xiān qù túshūguǎn, ránhòu qù Xīngbākè.
> I'll go to the library and then I'll go to Starbucks.
>
> Nǐ dàole dīshì zhàn, ránhòu yìzhí zǒu.
> After you get to the taxi stand, go straight.

6. jiù (see note 9, Chapter 8)

"Jiù" can be used to emphasize or confirm a fact: "this is exactly what the fact is."

For example:

> Bāshì zhàn jiù zài dàxué xiàomén duìmiàn.
> The bus stop is exactly across the street from the university gate.

7. zuò (see note 12, Chapter 3)

"Zuò" means "take" when it is used before a vehicle.

For example:

> zuò dìtiě   take the MTR
> zuò bāshì   take the bus

8. chū "to go through"

"Chū xiàomén" means "go through the university gate."

9. guò (see note 5, Chapter 7)

In the previous chapter, we learned that "guò" means "to spend (time), to celebrate (a birthday, a festival)," as in "guò shǔjià" "spend the summer vacation." Here, "guò" means "to cross." For example:

guò mǎlù   cross the street

10. zài······duìmiàn (see note 19, Chapter 2)

Previously, we learned the structure "subject + zài + p.w. + localizer." A localizer can be attached to a noun or a pronoun to form a place word. We have learned some localizers, such as "shàngbian" and "xiàbian." "Duìmiàn" is also a localizer that means "at the opposite side of." For example:

Bāshì zhàn jiù zài dàxué xiàomén duìmiàn.
The bus stop is just across the street from the university gate.

11. máfan (see note 5, Chapter 9)

In the previous chapter, we learned that "máfan" which means "troublesome, annoying" can be used as an adjective. For example:

Tāmen hěn máfan.
They are very annoying.

"Máfan" can also be used as a verb, meaning "to bother someone."

"Tài máfan nǐ le" means "I have bothered you so much." It is another way to show gratitude.

12. gěi + somebody + something

The verb "gěi" meaning "give" is followed by two objects, an indirect object and a direct object.

For example:

Tā gěi wǒ yì běn shū.
He gives me a book.

Wǒ tóngwū gěi wǒ yì zhāng diànhuà kǎ.
My roommate gives me a phone card.

13. zhǎo + nǐ + shíwǔ kuài

The verb "zhǎo," meaning "give change," can be also followed by two objects, an indirect object and a direct object.

For example:

Zhǎo nǐ shíwǔ kuài.
I'll give you $15 change.

Zhǎo tā bāshí kuài.
You give him $80 change.

14. nǎli nǎli

"Nǎli nǎli" means "I am flattered."

For example:

    A: Nǐ de Hànyǔ zhēn hǎo.
        Your Chinese is really good.
    B: Nǎli nǎli.
        I am flattered.
    A: Nǐ zuò de cài zhēn hǎo chī.
        Your cooking is very good.
    B: Nǎli nǎli.
        I am flattered.

Exercises

I. Listen to the dialog and choose the correct answer.

1. Tāmen zài nǎr?

    A. zài dìtiě shang   B. zài bāshì shang   C. zài dīshì shang

2. Xiānggǎng Dàxué zài nǎr?

    A. zài yínháng hòubian   B. zài yínháng pángbiān   C. zài bāshì zhàn hòubian

3. Yígòng duōshao qián?

    A. liùshí kuài   B. wǔshíyī kuài   C. wǔshíjiǔ kuài

II. Choose the correct words and fill in the blanks. Each word can be used only once.

dào   wǎng   chū   guò   zuò   jiù   gěi   zhǎo   máfan   ba

1. Nǐ děi _____ dìtiě qù Zhōnghuán.
2. Xīngbākè _____ zài túshūguǎn de hòubian.
3. Wǒ dài nǐ qù _____.
4. Yígòng sānshí qī kuài, nǐ _____ wǒ sìshí kuài, wǒ _____ nǐ sān kuài.
5. Dàbā, xiǎobā dōu _____ Zhōnghuán.
6. Tài _____ nǐ le!
7. _____ xiàomén, _____ mǎlù, _____ zuǒ guǎi, zài yìzhí zǒu.

III. Rearrange the words to form coherent sentences.

1. zài   wǒmen   yínháng   xiànzài   qiánbian   de

    _____.

2. chāoshì   zuǒ   dào   guǎi   wǎng   le

    _____.

3. bāshì zhàn   xiàomén   jiù   dàxué   duìmiàn   zài

    _____.

4. bāshì   děi   zhōnghuán   nǐ   qù   zuò

    _____.

5. nǎr   nín   dǎsuan   qǐng   qù   wèn

    _____.

IV. Answer the questions according to the picture.

1. Qǐngwèn, zěnme cóng Xiānggǎng Dàxué xiàomén qù túshūguǎn?
2. Qǐngwèn, zěnme cóng túshūguǎn qù sùshè?
3. Qǐngwèn, zěnme cóng Xiānggǎng Dàxué xiàomén qù bāshì zhàn?
4. Qǐngwèn, zěnme cóng bāshì zhàn qù Xiānggǎng Dàxué xiàomén?

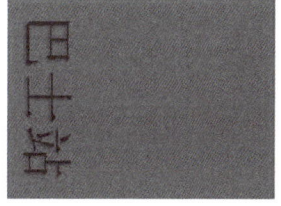
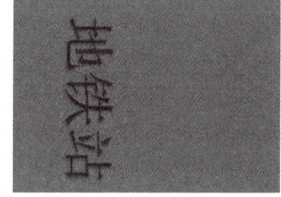

图书馆	túshūguǎn	library
超市	chāoshì	supermarket
餐厅	cāntīng	canteen
银行	yínháng	bank
宿舍	sùshè	dormitory
巴士站	bāshì zhàn	bus stop
地铁站	dìtiě zhàn	MTR station
香港大学校门	Xiānggǎng Dàxué xiàomén	the gate of the University of Hong Kong

Culture Note

Chinese Characters

Chinese characters constitute one of humanity's oldest systems of writing and have the most users in the world. There are many Chinese characters, totaling about 60,000 with about 6,000 basic ones. Chinese characters originate from pictures for keeping records. From ancient to modern times, the form and structure of Chinese characters has changed a lot, evolving from *jiaguwen*, *jinwen* (ancient language used in inscriptions on ancient bronze objects), *xiaozhuan* (small seal character), *lishu* (official script), and *kaishu* (regular script). The current script of Chinese characters is *kaishu* (regular script).

There are mainly four word-formation methods as follows:

Pictography (象形) refers to the method of drawing the form of a thing.

Self-explanatory (指事) characters are made by adding self-explanatory symbols on pictographs or are totally made of symbols.

Associative compounds (会意) are combinations of two or more symbols to represent a new character of a new meaning.

The pictophonetic method (形声) is a word-formation method combining one element of a character indicating meaning and the other, sound, into a new word. The form element indicates the word's meaning and characteristic. The phonetic element indicates the pronunciation of the word.

Chinese characters have been borrowed by Korea, Japan, and Vietnam, thereby promoting international communication. (214 words)

Ren Qiliang, ed., *Chinese Common Knowledge Series-Culture* (Hong Kong: Hong Kong China Tourism Press, 2005), 132.

第十课　请问，怎么去图书馆？

学生1：请问，怎么去图书馆？

学生2：（指着校园地图）这是校园地图。我们现在在银行的前边。你一直走，到了超市往左拐，然后，一直走。到了星巴克往右拐。图书馆就在星巴克的后边。

学生1：哦。我怎么去中环呢？

学生2：你得坐巴士去中环。你一直走，到了超市往右拐。出校门，过马路，巴士站就在大学校门对面。大巴、小巴都到中环。你也可以坐的士或者地铁，的士站就在巴士站旁边。

学生1：明白了。谢谢。

学生2：不客气。你现在打算去哪儿？

学生1：我先去图书馆。

学生2：我也去图书馆。我带你去吧。

学生1：太好了！太麻烦你了！

学生2：不客气。我们走吧。

【在的士上】

司机：您好，请问您去哪儿？

学生：您好，我要去中环地铁站，谢谢。

司机：好的，没问题。

【十分钟后】

司机：您到了。一共三十五块。

学生：好的，给您钱。

司机：您给我五十块，我找您十五块。您的汉语真好！

学生：哪里哪里。

Appendix 1
Introduction to Chinese characters

一、The strokes 笔画[1]

The strokes are the most basic part of Chinese characters. The typical strokes are as follows:

横 héng: 一
Examples: 一 (yī, one)、二 (èr, two)、三 (sān, three)

竖 shù: 丨
Example: 十 (shí, ten)

撇 piě: 丿
Examples: 人 (rén, person, people)、月 (yuè, moon, month)

捺 nà: ㇏
Example: 八 (bā, eight)

点 diǎn: 丶 ノ
Example: 小 (xiǎo, small, little)

提 tí: ✓
Example: 江 (jiāng, river)

折 zhé:

┐ example: 口 (kǒu, mouth)

∠ example: 么 (me, particle word)

∟ example: 出 (chū, out)

く example: 女 (nǚ, female)

∟ example: 四 (sì, four)

ᄔ example: 没 (méi, no)

ㄣ example: 专 (zhuān, special)

ㄋ example: 鼎 (dǐng, ancient vessel)

---

[1]. 古人书写汉字多用毛笔，所以落笔收笔均有笔锋，至今无论是印刷体还是手写体，汉字的一笔一画均有笔锋。笔锋使汉字更加刚劲有力，充满个性，初学者应该了解，但不必强求，更不要被其误导，认为一定要"画"出笔锋才是正确写法。Ancient Chinese people used brushes to write on silk and paper. The movement of the brush can be traced from the beginning to the end of each stroke for each different shape when the brush is pressed down, turned or lifted up, which is known as *bifeng*. Although most modern Chinese people do not use brushes to write, *bifeng* is carried forward to both printing and handwriting. The beginners should be aware of it but do not have to draw it.

ㄥ example: 凹 (āo, hollow)

㇆ example: 凸 (tū, raised)

㇇ example: 又 (yòu, again)

㇈ example: 及 (jí, and)

钩 gōu:

→ example: 买 (mǎi, buy)

亅 example: 小 (xiǎo, small, little)

ㄴ example: 以 (yǐ, use, take)

ㄟ example: 我 (wǒ, I, me)

亅 example: 了 (le, particle word)

㇆ example: 月 (yuè, month, moon)

㇆ example: 力 (lì, power)

㇈, ㄴ example: 也 (yě, also)

乚 example: 九 (jiǔ, nine)

㇉ example: 与 (yǔ, and)

㇂ example: 队 (duì, team)

ㄋ example: 课 (kè, class, lesson)

㇌ example: 乃 (nǎi, be, then)

㇁ example: 风 (fēng, wind)

二、The components 部件[2]

汉字的基本部件分为两种：独体字和非字部件。
There are two different kinds of components: independent and dependent.

独体字既可以成字，也可以作为合成字的部件。例如：人、口、木。
An independent component is a single character and can also form a part of compound characters, such as 人、口、木.

非字部件则只能作为合成字的部件。例如：亻、氵。
Dependent components can only be used as parts in compound characters, such as 亻、氵.

三、The structures 结构

汉字分为两大种：独体字和合成字。
All Chinese characters can be grouped into either single characters or compound characters.

独体字由笔画构成。例如：人、口、木。

---

2. 常用汉字一共有3,500个，覆盖了内地出版物用字99%以上，而合成大部分常用汉字的常用部件（独体字和非成字部件）也只不过380多个。因此，只要掌握了一部分常用部件，并掌握了汉字基本结构，学习汉字就不再是特别困难的事儿了。The frequently used Chinese characters are in total 3,500. They cover more than 99% of the characters used in modern publications on the Mainland. The parts used to assemble these characters are about 380, so it is important as well as efficient for learners to be aware of the components and the structure of Chinese characters from the outset.

Single characters are formed by strokes, such as 人、口、木.

合成字由两个或两个以上部件组合而成。例如：从、吕、众、仁。
Compound characters consist of two or more components, such as 从、吕、众、仁.

合成字遵循如下几条基本合成规律：
The basic rules of assembling a compound character with several parts are as follows:

  左右结构 left-right, 例如 examples: 林、你、进

  左中右结构 left-middle-right, 例如 examples: 谢

  上下结构 up-down, 例如 examples: 吕、森、看、庆

  上中下结构 up-middle-down, 例如 examples: 赢

  内外结构 outside-inside, 例如 examples: 回、国

四、The rules on the order of strokes 笔顺

The basic rules of writing a character stroke by stroke are as follows:

  先左后右 Left-right. Examples: 一、川、八、人、入、从

  先上后下 Up-down. Examples: 二、三、了、众、口、吕、品、看、庆

  先横后竖 Horizontal-vertical. Examples: 十、木、朩、林、森

  先外后内 Outside-inside. Examples: 月、冃、内

  先外后内再关闭 Outside-inside-bottom close. Examples: 日、回

  先左点后中和右上点 Dot: left first, middle and right last. Examples: 门、心、勺、犬

  特殊情况 Special case. Examples: 中、巾、小、女、匕、子、孑、也、阝

  辶最后写 Write last.

Appendix 2
Read and write Chinese characters

	#1				
	nǐ 你				
	you				

	#2				
	men 们				
	plural suffix				

	#3				
	hǎo 好				
	good				
你们好！Hello!					

	#4				
	wǒ 我				
	I; me				

Appendix 2

#5					
xìng 姓					
surname					

#6					
shì 是					
am; are; is					

#7					
hàn 汉					
Chinese (language)					

#8					
yǔ 语					
language					
汉语 Chinese language					

#9 #10				
lǎo shī 老 师				
teacher				

#11					
de 的					
possession / modification marker					

	#12				
	nín 您				
	you (in a respected way)				

	#13 #14				
	shén me 什 么				
	what				

	#15				
	yě 也				
	also				

	#16 #17				
	xué sheng 学 生				
	student				

	#16 #18				
	xué xí 学 习				
	study				

	#19 #20				
	míng zi 名 字				
	name				

#21	
jiào 叫	
to be called; call	

#22	
zhōng 中	
central; in the middle of	

#23	
guó 国	
country	
中国 China	

#24	
rén 人	
person/people	
中国人 Chinese people	

#25	
nǎ 哪	
which	

#26	
ma 吗	
a sentence particle to indicate a question	

Read and write Chinese characters 163

#27	bù	不				
		no				
#28	hěn	很				
		very				
#29 #30	fēi cháng	非常				
		extraordinarily				
		常常 often				
#31	máng	忙				
		busy				
#32	qǐng	请				
		please; to treat sb. to a meal, etc.				
#33	zuò	坐				
		sit; take (transportation tool)				

#34					
zhè 这					
this; these					

#35					
tā 他					
he; him					

#36					
tā 她					
she; her					

#37					
dōu 都					
both; all					

#38					
jiā 家					
home; family					

#39					
shéi 谁					
who; whom					

#40 bà 爸 father					

#41 mā 妈 mother					

#42 yǒu 有 has; have					

#43 jǐ 几 how many…					

#44 kǒu 口 measure word for the number of family members					

#45 yī 一 one					

#46					
èr 二					
two					

#47					
sān 三					
three					

#48					
sì 四					
four					

#49					
wǔ 五					
five					

#50					
liù 六					
six					

#51					
hé 和					
and					

	#52				
xiǎng 想					
miss somebody; want					

	#53				
nán 男					
male					

	#54 #55				
péng you 朋友					
friend					
男朋友 boyfriend 好朋友 good friend					

	#56				
gè 个					
general measure word					

	#57				
liǎng 两					
two (used before measure word)					

	#58				
méi 没					
have (no); (have) not					
没有 do not have					

Appendix 2

#59					
dà 大					
big					

#60 #61				
sù shè 宿舍				
dormitory				

#62 #14 #63			
zěn me yàng 怎么样			
how about			

#64					
nà 那					
that; those					

#65					
zhāng 张					
measure word for flat object					

#66					
bǐ 笔					
pen					

	#67				
	xiǎo 小				
	little; small				

	#68				
	zài 在				
	be at				

	#69 #70				
	zhuō zi 桌子				
	table; desk				

	#71 #72				
	shàng bian 上 边				
	upper side; above				

	#73				
	xià 下				
	下边 underneath				

	#74 #75				
	suī rán 虽然				
	although				

#76					
dàn 但					
but					
但是 but					

#77					
tài 太					
too					

#78					
luàn 乱					
messy					

#79					
le 了					
sentence particle					

#80					
shū 书					
book					

#81 ér 儿				
suffix				
这儿 here 那儿 there 哪儿 where				

#82 guì 贵				
expensive				

#83 #84 pián yi 便宜				
cheap				

#85 #86 duō shao 多少				
how much; how many				

#87 qián 钱				
money				

#88					
qī 七					
seven					

#89					
bā 八					
eight					

#90					
jiǔ 九					
nine					

#91					
shí 十					
ten					

#92					
kuài 块					
measure word for RMB					

#93					
mǎi 买					
buy					

	#94				
	hái 还				
	additionally; and also				

	#95				
	bǎi 百				
	hundred				

	#96				
	líng 零				
	zero				

	#97				
	máo 毛				
	measure word for RMB				

	#98				
	yòng 用				
	use				

	#99 #98 #100		
	xìn yòng kǎ 信 用 卡		
	credit card		

#101 #102				
piào liang 漂亮				
pretty; beautiful				

#103				
wèn 问				
ask				

#104				
qù 去				
go				

#105				
xiāng 香				
fragrant				

#106				
gǎng 港				
harbor				
香港 Hong Kong				

#107				
chī 吃				
eat				

#108				
fàn 饭				
meal				
吃饭 have a meal				

#109 #110				
jīn tiān 今 天				
today				

#111				
nán 难				
difficult				

#112 #113				
xǐ huan 喜 欢				
like				

#114 #115				
kā fēi 咖啡				
coffee				

#116				
hē 喝				
drink				

#117					
rè 热					
hot					
热咖啡 hot coffee					

#118					
huì 会					
know how to do something; will; shall; be going to . . .					

#119 #120				
yīng gāi 应该				
should				

#121					
jiāo 教					
teach					

#122					
měi 每					
every					
每天 every day					

#123 #124				
yīn wei 因为				
because				

#125 #126				
suǒ yǐ 所以				
so				

#127				
huā 花				
spend				

#128 #129				
shí jiān 时 间				
time				

#130 #131				
xīng qī 星 期				
week				

#132				
wǔ 午				
noon				
上午 morning 下午 afternoon				

#133					
zǎo 早					
early					
早上 morning 早饭 breakfast					

#134					
wǎn 晚					
late					
晚上 evening; night 晚饭 dinner					

#135					
diǎn 点					
o'clock; hour in the time point					

#136					
bàn 半					
half					

#137					
fēn 分					
minute					

#138				
kè 课				
class				
上课 go to class				

#139				
gēn 跟				
with				

#140				
shuō 说				
speak				
说汉语 speak Chinese				

#141 #142				
cān tīng 餐厅				
canteen; restaurant				

#143				
huí 回				
go back				

#144				
cóng 从				
from (place/ time point)				

#145				
dào 到				
to (place/time point); arrive				

#146 #147			
jué de 觉得			
feel; think			

#148				
běn 本				
measure word				

#149				
nǚ 女				
female				
女朋友 girlfriend				

#150				
kuài 筷				
chopsticks				
筷子 chopsticks				

#151 #152			
tóng wū 同屋			
roommate			

	#153				
nián 年					
	year				

	#154				
yuè 月					
	month				

	#155 #156				
má là 麻辣					
	hot and spicy				

	#157 #158				
Běi jīng 北京					
	Beijing				

	#159 #160				
cōng ming 聪明					
	clever; smart				

	#161				
gāo 高					
	tall				

#162					
shuài 帅					
handsome					

#163					
yòu 又					
again					
又……又 not only . . . but also					

#164					
shì 室					
room					

#165 #166					
bāng zhù 帮 助					
help					

#167					
hòu 候					
时候 time 有时候 sometimes					

#168					
xiě 写					
to write					

	#169 #170				
ér qiě 而且					
and					
不仅……而且 not only . . . but also					

	#171				
jiù 就					
exactly					

	#172				
kàn 看					
to look					

	#173				
lěng 冷					
cold					

	#174				
kè 客					
不客气 you are welcome					

	#175 #176				
gān shuǎng 干 爽					
cool and dry					

#177 #178				
gōng zuò 工 作				
job; to work				

#179				
qióng 穷				
poor				

#180				
xìng 兴				
高兴 happy				

#181				
qì 气				
天气 weather				

#182				
dōng 冬				
winter				
冬天 winter				

#183 #184				
shū fu 舒 服				
comfortable				

	#185				
	xià 夏				
	summer				
	夏天 summer				

	#186				
	zuì 最				
	most				

	#187				
	qiū 秋				
	autumn				
	秋天 autumn				

	#188 #189				
	liáng kuai 凉 快				
	cool				

	#190 #191				
	cháo shī 潮 湿				
	humid				

	#192				
	chūn 春				
	spring				
	春天 spring				

	#193 #194			
dǎ suan 打 算				
	plan			

	#195 #196			
nèi dì 内 地				
	mainland China			

	#197			
guò 过				
	spend			

	#198 #199			
shǔ jià 暑 假				
	summer vacation			

	#200 #201			
chéng shì 城 市				
	city			

	#202			
kě 可				
	可是 but			

#203 #204 dān xīn 担心 worry				

#205 tīng 听 hear				

#206 yǔ 雨 下雨 rainy				

#207 kōng 空 空气 air				

#208 shuǐ 水 water				

#175 #210 gān jìng 干净 clean				

#211				
bìng 病				
illness				

#212 #213 #70			
lā dù zi 拉肚子			
diarrhea			

#214				
sǐ 死				
dead				
死了 extremely				

#215				
xuě 雪				
snow				
下雪 snowy				

#216 #217			
jiàn kāng 健康			
healthy			

#218 #219			
yǐn chá 饮茶			
to drink tea and eat dim sum in Cantonese restaurants; yumcha			

	#220				
zhǐ 只					
only					

	#221 #222				
Guǎng dōng 广 东					
Guangdong Province					

	#223				
ér 而					
but					

	#224				
fāng 方					
北方 North China					

	#225				
tián 甜					
sweet					

	#226				
xián 咸					
salty					

#227					
bǐ 比					
compare to					

#228					
pà 怕					
可怕 scary					

#229					
ruǎn 软					
soft					

#230 #27 #231			
duì bu qǐ 对不起			
sorry			

#232					
xǐ 洗					
wash					

#233					
shǒu 手					
hand					

	#234					
	jī 鸡					
	chicken					

	#235					
	jiǎo 脚					
	feet					

	#236					
	zhǎo 爪					
	feet					

	#237					
	wèi 胃					
	stomach					

	#238					
	néng 能					
	able to					

	#239					
	xiā 虾					
	shrimp					

#222 #240				
dōng xi 东 西				
thing; stuff				

#241				
bāo 包				
bun				

#242				
huó 活				
生活 life				

#243 #244				
yuè dú 阅 读				
read				

#245				
zhōu 周				
week				
阅读周 reading week				

#246 #247				
fù mǔ 父 母				
parents				

Read and write Chinese characters 193

#248				
lái 来				
come				

#249 #250			
lǚ yóu 旅游			
travel			

#251				
xiān 先				
first				

#252				
zài 再				
again				

#253 #254 #255		
Tóng luó wān 铜锣湾		
Causeway Bay		

#256				
guàng 逛				
to stroll				

	#257 #258			
	shāng chǎng 商 场			
	shopping mall			

	#259 #260			
	hǎi yáng 海 洋			
	ocean			

	#261 #262			
	gōng yuán 公 园			
	park			
	海洋公园 Ocean Park			

	#263 #264			
	dòng wù 动 物			
	animal			

	#265 #266			
	má fan 麻 烦			
	annoyed; annoying			

	#267 #268			
	zhǔ yi 主 意			
	idea			

#269 dì 第				
number				

#270 dài 带				
take somebody to some place				

#271 wán 玩				
play				

#272 #273 shān dǐng 山顶				
the Peak				

#274 wéi 维				
维港 Victoria Harbor				

#275 jǐng 景				
海景 harbour view				

#276 xiān 鲜					
海鲜 seafood					

#277 xiào 校					
校园 campus					

#278 #80 #279 tú shū guǎn 图书馆				
library				

#280 #281 yín háng 银行				
bank				

#282 zhí 直					
straight					
一直 keep straight					

#283 zǒu 走					
walk					

#284 chāo 超					
超市 supermarket					

#285 wǎng 往					
toward					

#286 zuǒ 左					
left					

#287 guǎi 拐					
turn					
左拐 turn left					

#288 yòu 右					
right					
右拐 turn right					

#289 huán 环					
中环 Central					

#290					
chē 车	☐				
car					

#291					
chū 出	☐				
go out of					

#292					
mén 门	☐				
gate; door					
校门 school gate					

#293 #294					
mǎ lù 马路	☐ ☐				
street; road					

#295					
bā 巴	☐				
大巴 large bus 小巴 mini bus					

#296 #297					
duì miàn 对面	☐ ☐				
the opposite side					

#298 xiàn 现					
现在 now					

#299 zhǎo 找					
to give change					

#300 tí 题					
问题 question					

Index

The heading of an index entry in pinyin is followed by the Chinese character(s) and then chapter number.

B

ba, 吧, 3
bā, 八, 3
Bādátōng, 八达通, 3
bāshì, 巴士, 3
bàba, 爸爸, 2
bǎi, 百, 3
bàn, 半, 5
bāngzhù, 帮助, 6
běifāng, 北方, 8
Běijīng, 北京, 6
Běijīng kǎoyā, 北京烤鸭, 6
běn, 本, 3
bǐ, 比, 8
bǐ, 笔, 2
bīng, 冰, 4
búdàn……érqiě……, 不但……而且……, 6
búguò, 不过, 8
bú kèqi, 不客气, 3
bú shì……ér shì……, 不是……而是……, 8
bú shì……jiù shì……, 不是……就是……, 6
búyòng, 不用, 7
bù, 不, 1
bùtóng, 不同, 6

C

cài, 菜, 6
cāntīng, 餐厅, 4
cōngming, 聪明, 6
cóng……dào……, 从……到……, 5

CH

chā, 叉, 4
chāshāo bāo, 叉烧包, 8
chángchang, 尝尝, 8
chángcháng, 常常, 4
chāoshì, 超市, 10
cháoshī, 潮湿, 7
chéngshì, 城市, 7
chī fàn, 吃饭, 4
chū, 出, 10
chūntiān, 春天, 7

D

dǎsuan, 打算, 7
dà, 大, 2
dàbā, 大巴, 10
dà fó, 大佛, 9
Dàyǔshān, 大屿山, 9
dài, 带, 9
dānxīn, 担心, 7
dànshì, 但是, 2
dāo, 刀, 4
dào, 到, 6
……de huà, jiù……, ……的话,就……, 4
děi, 得, 4
dì, 第, 9
dìdi, 弟弟, 2
dìtiě, 地铁, 3
dìtú, 地图, 10
dì-yī tiān, 第一天, 9
diǎn, 点, 5
diǎnxin, 点心, 8
diànhuà kǎ, 电话卡, 3
diànyǐng, 电影, 5
Dīng, 丁, 1
dōngtiān, 冬天, 7
dōngxi, 东西, 2
dòngwù, 动物, 9
dōu, 都, 2
duìbuqǐ, 对不起, 8
duìmiàn, 对面, 10
duōshǎo qián, 多少钱, 3

E

èr, 二, 1

F

fǎlǜ, 法律, 1
fānqié, 番茄, 4
fēicháng, 非常, 1
fēn, 分, 5
fēngwèi, 风味, 6
fèngzhǎo, 凤爪, 8
fùmǔ, 父母, 9

G

gāo, 高, 6
gāoxìng, 高兴, 1
gānjìng, 干净, 7
gānshuǎng, 干爽, 7
gēge, 哥哥, 2
gè, 个, 2
gěi, 给, 8
gēn, 跟, 5
gēn……bù yíyàng, 跟……不一样, 8
gōngzuò, 工作, 1
Guǎngdōng, 广东, 8
guàng, 逛, 9
guì, 贵, 3
guó, 国, 1
guò, 过, 7, 10

H

hái, 还, 3
háishi, 还是, 3
hǎijǐng, 海景, 9
hǎixiān, 海鲜, 9
Hǎiyáng Gōngyuán, 海洋公园, 9
Hànyǔ, 汉语, 1
Hànzì, 汉字, 6
hǎo, 好, 1
hǎo chī, 好吃, 4
hǎo de, 好的, 3
hǎo hē, 好喝, 4
hǎo ma, 好吗, 4
hào, 号, 3
hé, 和, 2
héfěn, 河粉, 4
hěn, 很, 1
hóngsè, 红色, 2
hòubian, 后边, 3
huā, 花, 5
huài, 坏, 4
huí, 回, 5
huì, 会, 7
huì, 会, 4
huǒguō, 火锅, 6
huòzhě, 或者, 3

J

jī, 鸡, 8
jí le, 极了, 6
jǐ, 几, 2
jǐ diǎn, 几点, 5
jiā, 家, 2
jiārén, 家人, 2
jiànkāng, 健康, 8
jiāo, 教, 4
jiāohuàn shēng, 交换生, 5
jiǎo, 脚, 8
jiào, 叫, 1
jiàoshì, 教室, 6
jiějie, 姐姐, 2
jīntiān, 今天, 4
jìn, 进, 2
jìn, 近, 3
jīngjì, 经济, 1
jiǔ, 九, 3
jiǔ, 酒, 5
jiǔyuè, 九月, 6
jiù, 就, 10
juéde, 觉得, 5

K

kāfēi, 咖啡, 4
kǎ, 卡, 3
kàn, 看, 5
kěpà, 可怕, 8
kěshì, 可是, 7
kè, 刻, 5
kōngqì, 空气, 7
kǒu, 口, 2
kuài, 块, 3
kuàizi, 筷子, 4

L

lā dùzi, 拉肚子, 7
là, 辣, 6
lái, 来, 9
Lánguìfāng, 兰桂坊, 5
lǎoshī, 老师, 1
lèi, 累, 5
lěng, 冷, 7
lǐ, 里, 6
lǐbian, 里边, 4
liángkuai, 凉快, 7
liǎng, 两, 2
liáo tiānr, 聊天儿, 5
líng, 零, 3
liù, 六, 2
luàn, 乱, 2
lǚyóu, 旅游, 9

M

ma, 吗, 1
māma, 妈妈, 2
má, 麻, 6
máfan, 麻烦, 9
mǎlù, 马路, 10
mǎi, 买, 3
máng, 忙, 2
máo, 毛, 3
méiyǒu, 没有, 2
méiyou, 没有, 7
měi, 美, 1
Měiguó, 美国, 1
měi tiān, 每天, 5
mèimei, 妹妹, 2
mén, 门, 10
miàn, 面, 4
miànbāo, 面包, 2
míng, 明, 1
míngbai le, 明白了, 3
míngzi, 名字, 1

N

nǎ, 哪, 1
nǎli nǎli, 哪里哪里, 10
nà, 那, 2
nǎichá, 奶茶, 4
nán, 难, 1
nán, 男, 2
nán chī, 难吃, 4
nán péngyou, 男朋友, 2
Nányādǎo, 南丫岛, 9

nǎr, 哪儿, 3
nàr, 那儿, 4
ne, 呢, 1
nèidì, 内地, 7
néng, 能, 8
nǐ kàn, 你看, 2
nǐmen, 你们, 1
nǐmen de, 你们的, 1
nín, 您, 1
niúròu, 牛肉, 4
nǔlì, 努力, 5
nǚ péngyou, 女朋友, 5

O
ò, 哦, 4

P
pāi, 拍, 8
pángbiān, 旁边, 3
píjiǔ, 啤酒, 3
piányi, 便宜, 3
piàoliang, 漂亮, 2
píng, 瓶, 3

Q
qī, 七, 3
Qī-shíyī (7-11), 七十一 (7-11), 3
qíguài, 奇怪, 4
qián, 钱, 3
qiánbian, 前边, 3
qié-dàn sānwénzhì, 茄蛋三文治, 4
qiézi, 茄子, 4
qīngsōng, 轻松, 5
qǐng, 请, 2
qǐng, 请, 4
qǐng wèn, 请问, 3
qióng, 穷, 7
qiūtiān, 秋天, 7
qùnián, 去年, 6
qù, 去, 3

R
ránhòu, 然后, 5
rè, 热, 4
rén, 人, 1
rènshi, 认识, 1
ruǎn, 软, 8

S
sān, 三, 2
sǐ le, 死了, 7
sì, 四, 2
Sìchuān, 四川, 6
sìyuè, 四月, 7
sùshè, 宿舍, 2
suīrán, 虽然, 2
suǒyǐ, 所以, 5

SH
shālǜ, 沙律, 8
Shāndǐng, 山顶, 9
shāngchǎng, 商场, 9
shàngbian, 上边, 2
shàng kè, 上课, 5
shàngwǔ, 上午, 5
shéi, 谁, 2
shénme, 什么, 1
shēng bìng, 生病, 7
shēnghuó, 生活, 5
shí, 十, 3
shíjiān, 时间, 5
shíyuè, 十月, 7
shì, 是, 1
shì de, 是的, 1
shìshi, 试试, 8
shǒujī, 手机, 2
shū, 书, 2
shūfu, 舒服, 7
shǔjià, 暑假, 7
shuài, 帅, 6
shuǐ, 水, 7
shuìjiào, 睡觉, 5
shuō, 说, 5

T
tā, 他, 2
tā, 她, 2
tāmen, 他们, 2
Tàiguó, 泰国, 9
tài……le, 太……了, 2
tài hǎo le, 太好了, 4
tài máfan nǐ le, 太麻烦你了, 10
tèbié, 特别, 9
tiānqì, 天气, 7
tián, 甜, 8
tīngshuō, 听说, 7
tǐng……de, 挺……的, 1
Tóngluówān, 铜锣湾, 9
tóngwū, 同屋, 6
túshūguǎn, 图书馆, 5

W
wàzi, 袜子, 2
wàibian, 外边, 4
wǎnshang, 晚上, 4
wǎng, 往, 10
Wáng, 王, 1
wánr, 玩儿, 9
Wéigǎng, 维港, 9
wèi, 胃, 8
wèi shénme, 为什么, 5
wénhuà, 文化, 5
wèn, 问, 3
wèntí, 问题, 10
wǒ, 我, 1
wúliáo, 无聊, 9
wǔ, 五, 2

X
Xīgòng, 西贡, 9
xǐhuan, 喜欢, 4
xǐshǒujiān, 洗手间, 8
xiājiǎo, 虾饺, 8
xiàbian, 下边, 2
xià ge xīngqī, 下个星期, 9
xiàtiān, 夏天, 7

xiàwǔ, 下午, 5
xià xuě, 下雪, 7
xià yǔ, 下雨, 7
xiān……zài……, 先……再……, 9
xián, 咸, 8
xiànjīn, 现金, 3
xiànzài, 现在, 10
Xiānggǎng Dàxué, 香港大学, 3
xiǎng, 想, 2
xiǎng, 想, 3
xiào, 校, 10
xiǎobā, 小巴, 10
xiàoyuán, 校园, 10
xiě, 写, 6
xièxie, 谢谢, 2
xìnyòng kǎ, 信用卡, 3
Xīngbākè, 星巴克, 4
xīngqītiān, 星期天, 5
xīngqīwǔ, 星期五, 5
xīngqīyī, 星期一, 5
xìng, 姓, 1
xuéqī, 学期, 9
xuésheng, 学生, 1
xuéxí, 学习, 1
xuéyǒu, 学友, 6

Y

yě, 也, 1
yèjǐng, 夜景, 9
yī, 一, 1
yí ge rén, 一个人, 9
yígòng, 一共, 3
yǐzi, 椅子, 2
yìbiān……yìbiān……, 一边……一边……, 5
yìqǐ, 一起, 6
yìzhí, 一直, 10
yīnwei, 因为, 5
yínháng, 银行, 10
yǐn chá, 饮茶, 8
yīnggāi, 应该, 4
Yīngguó, 英国, 1
yòng, 用, 3
yǒu, 有, 2
yǒu de……yǒu de……, 有的……有的……, 8
yǒudiǎnr, 有点儿, 7
yǒu míng, 有名, 8
yǒu qián, 有钱, 7
yǒu shíhou, 有时候, 6
yǒu yìsi, 有意思, 1
yòu, 右, 10
yòu……yòu……, 又……又……, 6
yuǎn, 远, 3
yuèdú zhōu, 阅读周, 9
yúntūn, 云吞, 4

Z

zázhì, 杂志, 3
zài, 在, 2
zài……de shíhou, 在……的时候, 7
zàijiàn, 再见, 1
zǎoshang, 早上, 5
zěnme, 怎么, 3
zěnme yàng, 怎么样, 2
zǒu, 走, 10
zuì, 最, 7
zuìhǎo, 最好, 8
zuǒ, 左, 10
zuǒ guǎi, 左拐, 10
zuò, 坐, 2
zuò, 坐, 3
zuò, 做, 4

ZH

zhàn, 站, 3
zhāng, 张, 2
Zhāng, 张, 6
zhǎo, 找, 10
zhàopiàn, 照片, 2
zhè, 这, 2
zhēn, 真, 7
zhěntou, 枕头, 2
zhèr, 这儿, 3
zhī, 只, 2
zhǐ, 只, 8
Zhōng cāntīng, 中餐厅, 5
Zhōngguó, 中国, 1
Zhōnghuán, 中环, 10
zhǔyi, 主意, 9
zhuānyè, 专业, 1
zhuōzi, 桌子, 2